Shaun Lambert has thought deeply about what makes people into effective and spiritually integrated human beings, drawing on biblical wisdom and insights from psychology. This is a book full of treasures and I commend it warmly.

Mark Woods, consulting editor, The Methodist Recorder *and formerly editor,* The Baptist Times

A Book of Sparks is an essential read, both for those who are seeking to realise the deep peace Jesus has given them and for those involved in pastoral and healing ministries within the church. Shaun brilliantly reveals the gift of paying attention to the present (in line with Jesus' teaching from Matthew 6). This book will keep the church from mistakenly discarding a God-given ability because of the cultural connotations that are often applied to it. Illuminating, refreshing and orthodox: I recommend it highly.

Revd Will Van Der Hart, Director of Mind and Soul, Pastoral Chaplain HTB

Shaun Lambert has been an attentive listener to God's word. He absorbed the principles and practice of *Lectio Divina* from the Benedictine monastic tradition through silence, solitude and mindful listening, particularly in the monastery Church of Worth Abbey. He has passed on the ancient monastic wisdom he found through this experience in the pages of this book and in retreats has led. He is known here as 'the Benedictine Baptist' because of his faithfulness and attentiveness to God's wisdom, amply expressed in these chapters so that others, in this present age, may benefit.

Fr. Patrick Fludder, Subprior and Abbey Bursar, formerly Director of Worth Abbey † The Open Cloister

About the author

Shaun Lambert is a Baptist minister in Stanmore, NW London. He is part of the New Wine leader's network, and PREMIER Mind and Soul network.

For more than ten years he studied integrative and relational counselling at Roehampton University. He writes regularly for the *Baptist Times*. He believes that all truth is God's truth and that Christians need to be learners and thinkers who help critique and transform culture.

Shaun is currently researching a PhD in New Testament studies and psychology focusing on watchfulness in Mark's gospel and its relation to mindfulness

He is married to Clare and has two children, Zachary and Amy, and a dog called Coco.

Shaun Lambert is the Senior Minister of Stanmore Baptist Church, Abercorn Road, Stanmore, Middx, HA7 2PH. He can be contacted by email on shaun@stanmorebc.co.uk. You can visit his website at http://shaunlambert.co.uk/.

A Book of Sparks

A Study in Christian Mind*Full*ness

Second edition

Shaun Lambert

instant
ap☐stle

First published in Great Britain in 2012. This edition published 2014.

Instant Apostle
The Barn
1 Watford House Lane
Watford
Herts
WD17 1BJ

British Library Cataloguing-in-Publication Data

A catalogue record for this book is available from the British Library

This book and all other Instant Apostle books are available from Instant Apostle:

Website: www.instantapostle.com
E-mail: info@instantapostle.com

ISBN 978-1-909728-15-8

Printed in Great Britain

Instant Apostle is a new way of getting ideas flowing, between followers of Jesus, and between those who would like to know more about His Kingdom.

It's not just about books and it's not about a one-way information flow. It's about building a community where ideas are exchanged. Ideas will be expressed at an appropriate length. Some will take the form of books. But in many cases ideas can be expressed more briefly than in a book. Short books, or pamphlets, will be an important part of what we provide. As with pamphlets of old, these are likely to be opinionated, and produced quickly so that the community can discuss them.

Well-known authors are welcome, but we also welcome new writers. We are looking for prophetic voices, authentic and original ideas, produced at any length; quick and relevant, insightful and opinionated. And as the name implies, these will be released very quickly, either as Kindle books or printed texts or both.

Join the community. Get reading, get writing and get discussing!

Having been disciplined a little, they will receive great good, because God tested them and found them worthy of himself; like gold in the furnace he tried them, and like a sacrificial burnt offering he accepted them. In the time of their visitation they will shine forth, and will run like sparks through the stubble. (*Apocrypha,* Wisdom 3:5-7 RSV)

Acknowledgements and Dedication

I have been very blessed to learn in so many directions from so many people who have encouraged me to write and to be watchful. I'd like to express my gratitude to Gold Hill Baptist Church, Spurgeon's College and New Wine for spiritual formation over the last 25 years.

In particular, with regard to my writing, I would like to acknowledge the part played by Mark Woods when he was the Editor of *The Baptist Times*, who inspired me to develop my thinking into articles. This book is shaped by his editing skills. Simon Walker read some of my writing and encouraged me to put it into book form, and also helped me to develop my thinking.

Simon Barrington-Ward, in his compelling little book *The Jesus Prayer* and in conversation, got me hooked on contemplation. The monks of Worth Abbey have enabled me to explore *Lectio Divina*, silence and solitude in their beautiful Abbey Church.

I have been compelled to study Mark's gospel, having had my eyes opened to its mysterious complexity by Crispin Fletcher-Louis. Will Van der Hart has offered profound commentary on what I have written and has been a great conversation partner.

Professor Guy Claxton has also fostered my interest in the learning sciences, both in his writing and in conversation. Nicki Copeland has beautifully copy edited various manuscripts, along with my father, Nigel Lambert.

I am very grateful to Stanmore Baptist Church for loving my family, and to the men's group for throwing themselves into trialling the concepts in the book.

Clare, my wife, has encouraged me to be mindful of my family and helped me to think outside the box. Zac and Amy, our children, have shown me how love and relationship is at the heart of all goodness. Coco, our dog, has shown me the importance and joy of free running.

I'd like to thank my father for showing us the world, and my mother for teaching me to read at the age of three, and my brother, sister and wider family for being there.

And thanks to Liz Jordan for her listening and seeing.

In this new edition I would particularly like to thank Sarah Marten for her encouragement and help to run courses, and to have a new edition and a study guide. I would also like to thank the folk from St Mary's Ealing who came on the courses organised by Sarah, and who helped shape the study guide and some of the changes in this edition.

Contents

Foreword

When I first read Shaun Lambert's draft of *A Book of Sparks*, I found the experience akin to a train journey. I felt I was travelling with a wise friend through an unfolding landscape. My friend was a resident in the land and wanted to take me on a journey so that he could point out its wonders and features, through the train window, along the way.

As we travelled, he generously shared the names and addresses of other guides who lived in various parts of the land. These wise folk themselves knew the routes up hills and down valleys. He introduced me to the places where some of those paths started, showing me how to return to them, what I would need to begin to travel and what I could expect to find as I made my own journey. I was left intrigued by not only the landscape, but by its other inhabitants too.

The train travelled purposefully with steady pace; thus my glimpse of the vistas was relatively brief but also beguiling. I knew I wanted to return. But the choice to do so and the work of doing so, would be mine.

As a journey, *A Book of Sparks* is an enriching and unfolding experience. Like any wise guide, Shaun has learned the art of giving just enough but not too much detail about any one site we pass by. He knows that we must discover in our own way and our own time the route into the land itself. He is not afraid to make wide and sometimes apparently disconnected observations about aspects of the landscape. Education, physical geography, work patterns, economics, emotional health and art all come within his range. Some of these observations have the character of personal opinion, personal politics almost. But even these are offered with gentle weight, opening rather than closing discussion. Implicit within this wide scope is the conviction that there is no area of the landscape – of life – that is outside the reach of God.

The route is determined by the train track itself; and for Shaun, this is Mark's gospel. Relatively few contemporary books attempt to work pastorally from the text of an entire biblical book. We have tended to prefer to roam, picking our themes from a broader range of authorial perspective. By attaching us so firmly to the skeleton of Mark's language and thought, Shaun forces us to relook at old, familiar and worn passages with fresh sight. One of the explicit appeals he makes to us is that looking – really looking, which includes really seeing, really hearing – is a decisive action we must relearn if we are to surrender to the true power of the biblical text. Shaun is concerned with helping us become, in the language of Mark's Jesus, 'watchful'; and watchfulness is a demanding if rewarding discipline that lies at the heart of Christian discipleship.

I enjoy travel books; the gentle and heart-warming companionship of someone who can open up a new landscape, perhaps doing most of the work for us. I know I read them lazily. In the end, Shaun turned out to be not such an undemanding tour guide. Kindly but firmly, I was made to look at myself and my practice. There are disciplines here and these require work.

A Book of Sparks, like Mark's gospel, provokes response. For the spiritually diffident, it challenges us to work harder at our engagement with our bodies, our neighbours, our feelings, our Bibles. Like Mark's gospel, it is concrete, written about the everyday. God is found in the here and now. Like Mark, Shaun wants us to encounter a love in God that penetrates all aspects of our selves – to repair parts of us which are broken and to re-find pieces that have been lost. In contrast to some of the literature with which Shaun dialogues, the goal to our well-being is not emptiness but fullness; attachment as opposed to detachment. Ultimately, his goal, I believe, is to lead us to an encounter with a God who is incarnate and who invites us to find our fullness of life in Him.

Simon Walker
March 2012

Author's note: Entering into full relationship

This book has come out of my personal journey. I have realised that if I want to change the world, or the church, I need to begin with changing myself. The way God has changed me is through relationship.

We sat beside the window looking out over the snowy Oxfordshire fields. After about half an hour the leader of the course said, 'I think you are carrying a lot of sadness and have carried it for a long time.'

Looking at me, no one would have guessed this. Maybe it had leaked from the hidden emotional part of me. Right at that moment it was as if light broke through the window from God and I became aware of the sadness.

It belonged to part of me but it wasn't all of me. I decided not to deny it but to acknowledge it, and as I did, it was as though just as snowflakes were falling outside, inside the cold flakes of sadness began to rise and leave me.

I was on a week-long Undefended Leadership course at Ripon College, Cuddesdon, led by the Revd Simon Walker. This was the defining moment of the week for me: I chose to be undefended but not defenceless. I was helped in that moment by being in real relationship with someone else who had wisdom and insight to help me.

But being undefended is about a wider awareness, not just of our fears and insecurities but also our creative, gifted self. Very often we deny this aspect of our self, so keen are we not to downplay our sinful nature.

In dialectical therapy, which is a mindfulness-incorporating therapy, it is acknowledged that we have a thinking mind and a feeling mind. For instance, with our feeling mind we might foster our children's dependency on us, and with our thinking mind we might force autonomy on them. When we bring the two together we access what is called our 'wise' mind, in which we give space for dependency and autonomy.

If psychotherapy can help people who are not Spirit-bearing Christians to access their 'wise' mind, how much more should we as Christians enable this for ourselves and others? When Solomon asked for the gift of a wise mind, it touched every aspect of his being.

Being undefended is accepting ourselves as we are while being 100 per cent committed to changing into Christ's likeness. It is recognising that the new self that Ephesians talks about is not all mixed up with our old self, but is a separate, present and clear reality.

The Bible is very clear about this. Old and new selves are separate identities. Light separates from darkness. We can access the new self and the light right now.

Sadly we have forgotten this reality. When we ask, 'Yes, but how do I access this reality?' we do not know the answer. We are to be transformed by the renewing of our minds, but our minds are untrained. Not only that but our minds are often fixed. We avoid new experiences and spaces, and we are full of bitterness because we have fixed opinions: 'Bad things should never happen to me,' for instance, and we are at the mercy of rigid thinking like, 'I already know the answer.' This is a form of mindlessness.

But if our minds are not fixed, we are at the mercy of urges which are part of the pattern of this world: I will have one more cigarette, drink, chocolate bar, one more look at that website, and so on.

The Spirit of wisdom is explained by fluid metaphors: wind, fire, water, spirit. This fluid Spirit of wisdom and revelation enables us to avoid the extremes of a fixed mind or a mind of uncontrollable urges. And thus we can find an undefended middle path.

Of course sin tries to fix us down, nail us to our habits. The devil tried to fix Jesus down, nail Him permanently – but the devil couldn't hold Him. One of the great truths of the cross is that sin can no longer hold us down. Darkness cannot extinguish the light of our new self.

In this introduction I have touched on different relationships we have. In this book, I want to focus on five overlapping and interlocking relationships. These are archetypal human relationships, which psychologists have recognised and mapped. Petruska Clarkson was one of the first to recognise and lay out their interconnectedness.[1]

I have taken them back to their archetypal and spiritual basis in our ordinary human lives. The attention and awareness I am asking you to develop is, in part, your relational awareness – trying to see these five relationships at work in your own life.

- The first, which inhabits everything we do, is the spiritual relationship, with God, others and the world.

- We then need to establish real relationships, where we are a person and treat others as people. We do not need to be friends with everyone, but we do need to be authentic.

- None of our relationships grow unless we work at them, unless we form bonds and alliances with God, others and ourselves. And so we need working relationships.

- As we know, many relationships exist in a distorted way. These need to brought into the light and restored to health. Jesus Himself was seen in a distorted way by the disciples and the religious leaders, as a political Messiah, rather than the Messiah of the kingdom.

---

[1] Petruska Clarkson, *The Therapeutic Relationship* (London: Whurr Publishers Ltd, 1995).

- Finally, we are all wounded in some way – and we need to be a repairer of relationships, and enter into repairing relationships.

These archetypal relationships are at work in Mark's gospel and can help us frame a view of personal and community discipleship that transforms our lives and communities.

A Book of Sparks now has a more in-depth introduction to mindfulness at the beginning, as well as 40 days of meditations which are to be read slowly and mindfully – one each day.

The book is designed to be used over a 40-day period, with a short chapter to be read each day. Forty days is a significant number, biblically and psychologically, in terms of producing change in us. It could be used for Lent or another period of self-examination.

Each week we will consider aspects of the five relationships we need to transform, along with a reflection from Mark's gospel. These five relationships will be considered as we look at wider perspectives on the world: psychology, business, our relationships, ecology and so on. Looking at different perspectives helps develop our awareness and attention. This is mindful learning; too often we are stuck in one perspective.

Ellen Langer is famous for her research on mindfulness without meditation, which she has been doing for the last 40 years. She came up with the term 'mindfulness' independently of its introduction to psychology from Buddhist thought and practice, and without herself being influenced by this other strand.

Langer says that mindfulness is the ordinary everyday capacity each of us has to notice new things. This is a deceptively simple idea. She arrived at the concept of mindfulness because she was studying what she calls 'mindlessness'.

What is mindlessness? Langer defines mindlessness as,

characterized by an entrapment in old categories; by automatic behaviour that precludes attending to new signals; and by action that operates from a single perspective.[2]

If you already know about mindfulness in cognitive psychology or Buddhism, your mind may well be making connections between what Ellen Langer says and what you have come across elsewhere. In the mindfulness used in cognitive psychology, we are also asked to observe and become aware of mindless automatic thinking.

Ellen Langer's work is a significant piece of research that points towards mindfulness as a universal human capacity. This universal human capacity is to be distinguished from the mindful awareness practices that enable us to access a mindful state. For Ellen Langer, the primary mindful awareness practice is the ordinary capacity of noticing. She uses her concept of mindlessness to help her define her version of mindfulness:

A mindful approach to any activity has three categories; the continuous creation of new categories; openness to new information; and an implicit awareness of more than one perspective.[3]

We are called to be in the world, but not of the world – and also to read the world for God's many-sided truth and wisdom.

Mark's gospel is all about relationship, community, family and discipleship, but above all it is about 'watchfulness'. This is spelt out explicitly in chapters 13 and 14, but is implicit in the rest of the gospel. 'Watchfulness' was once considered the

---

[2] Ellen Langer, *The Power of Mindful Learning* (Addison-Wesley Publishing, 1997) p.4.
[3] Ibid, p.4.

hallmark of being a disciple, but now it has dropped off our horizon. It is something Jesus modelled in the Garden of Gethsemane and elsewhere, and He commands all disciples to be watchful (Mark 13:37). If Jesus believes it to be important then it must be. I will try and address the question as to 'why' you should take it seriously, as well as the question 'What does it mean and how do I do it?'

I believe that watchfulness, as the hallmark of being a disciple, is ripe for reintroducing to the mainstream. An overlapping concept in psychology called mindfulness, which is present-moment awareness, is becoming increasingly mainstream. Psychological science is mapping out the benefits of such attentiveness. Buddhism is attracting a lot of focus because of its version(s) of mindfulness. Christian contemplative practice needs to be brought out into the open and into the marketplace. I would call this Christian contemplative practice 'mind*Full*ness', because our being is filled with the awareness of the presence of God. As Paul prays in Ephesians 3:19, we are to be 'filled to the measure of all the fulness of God'. It is the right time for the church to rediscover the power of contemplative evangelism as well as deepening its own discipleship path.

If you are suffering from the universal vulnerability of stress then it would be helpful, alongside the contemplative practices I am introducing here, to explore the mindful awareness practices within secular psychologies, like attending to your breath, the body scan, eating raisins mindfully and so on. The breath, the body, the raisin, become something we focus our attention on in the present moment. As our mind wanders we bring it back to the focus of attention, in a noticing, compassionate, non-judgemental way. We are moving from narrative thinking to an experiential sense of self through our senses.

The best way to understand these mindful awareness practices is to start doing them! There is a lot we can do to help ourselves. There is a link at the end of the book to some free meditations.

More serious conditions and psychological distress, such as depression and anxiety, can also be helped through mindfulness-based or mindfulness-incorporating therapies. These should be done holistically in consultation with your doctor or counsellor.

An introduction to mindfulness

The origin of the word

The word 'mindfulness' is a sixteenth-century English term that is used to translate Buddhist technical terms. So says Rupert Gethin in his article 'On some definitions of mindfulness'.[4]

It is not surprising then, with this Oxford English Dictionary reference to the date 1530, that the King James Version of the Bible published in 1611 has the word 'mindful' in it a number of times. For example, 'What is man, that thou art **mindful** of him? and the son of man, that thou visitest him?' (Psalm 8:4, emphasis added). Being mindful of God is becoming aware of when He 'visitest' us.

My introduction to mindfulness

Imagine that you are not in England on a cold autumn day but in Paris on a warm spring day. You are sitting in a street cafe, with someone you love beside you, perhaps with your young children playing in the square in front of you. You have a cup of coffee or a glass of beer or wine to savour slowly. It is a perfect doorway into the present moment, and into present-moment awareness, which is mindfulness.

But you can't enter that doorway because you are in a limited place, a place limited by anxiety, fear and stress. Your mind is elsewhere, ruminating negatively about something in the past or something in the future.

Seven years ago I was in that place and unable to enter that beautiful doorway into the present moment and into the lives of those around me, because of stress.

---

[4] *Contemporary Buddhism* Vol. 12, No. 1, May 201, p.263 .

Martin Laird (OSA) in his wise book *Into the Silent Land: The Practice of Contemplation* says that in order to enter that doorway into the present moment, we need to be able to answer this riddle: Am I my thoughts and feelings? Are you your thoughts and feelings?[5]

The central insight of mindfulness – and Buddhists, Christians and psychologists all agree on this – is that we are bigger than our thoughts and feelings; they are discrete events in our minds. We can observe our thoughts and feelings and decentre from them. We might want to say from a Christian perspective that they are part of us, but they are not us.

This is very important because if we are totally identified with our thoughts and see them as a direct readout of reality, then we become the victim of our thoughts and not the witness of them. We react automatically to our thoughts rather than responding compassionately. But instead of looking at life *from* our thoughts, we can look *at* our thoughts.

For example, in Romans 12:2, Paul tells us, 'Do not conform any longer to the pattern of this world, but be transformed by the renewing of your mind.' Our thoughts and feelings are often shaped by our culture into narcissistic, competitive, fearful or consumerist patterns. This verse enables us to witness our thoughts and enables us to decentre from them.

Paul follows this up in 2 Corinthians 10:5, where he says, 'take captive every thought to make it obedient to Christ.' This verse also enables us to disarm our thoughts – to notice them, but to let them go.

Mindfulness is not about avoiding difficult reality, but about facing it head on.

Mark's gospel also tells us that we don't see clearly. At the beginning of the gospel Jesus tells people to repent; the word *metanoiete* is about having a new mind. The verses above are verses that we will keep coming back to, and I will restate

---

[5] Martin Laird, *Into The Silent Land* (London: DLT, 2006) p.77.

their central insight throughout the book, until through this repetition the truth sinks into our consciousness.

In Mark 4 there is a small kingdom parable that takes up the theme of the more famous 'seed and the sower' parable which it follows. It begins with the idea of bringing in a lamp: 'Do you bring in a lamp to put it under a bowl or a bed?' (Mark 4:21).

The lamp, like the seed, refers to the Word of God. Psalm 119:105 says, 'Your word is a lamp to my feet and a light for my path.' In the one reality we all experience there is a hidden spiritual dimension. One day, says Jesus, what is hidden will be revealed (Mark 4:22).

Because of the hidden nature of this spiritual reality, Jesus' constant refrain is, 'If anyone has ears to hear, let them hear' (Mark 4:23). That is a clue to us that our perceiving of reality is not automatic, or necessarily right.

Jesus underlines this in the next verse (v.24), which reads literally in the Greek, '*See* what you hear.' The Greek word here is *blepete*, which is used repeatedly throughout Mark's gospel as a word about watchfulness and spiritual perception.

It was contemplative practices seven years ago that enabled me to find the doorway to present-moment awareness and to decentre from my afflictive thoughts and feelings. Soon after that day in Paris, whilst on sabbatical, a small book called *The Jesus Prayer* by Simon Barrington-Ward, former Bishop of Coventry, leapt off the shelf at me.[6] This ancient, repetitive, contemplative prayer, said with the breath goes, 'Lord Jesus Christ, Son of God, have mercy on me, a sinner.' It enabled me to decentre from my anxious thoughts and enter into the healing presence of God.

At the same time I was studying counselling and psychotherapy at Roehampton University and came upon mindfulness in psychology. Mindfulness as present-moment

---

[6] Simon Barrington-Ward, *The Jesus Prayer* (Oxford: BRF, 2007).

awareness is a universal human capacity, and it can be arrived at through mindful awareness or meditative practices. Within modern psychology these practices have Buddhist roots, although they are not religious or spiritual but entirely reality focused. They include attending to the breath, the mindful eating of a something like a raisin, and mindful walking.

As I was researching mindfulness in psychology and the Jesus Prayer, I came across the writings of Diadochus of Photike, a fifth-century Bishop who was instrumental in developing the Jesus Prayer. One quote in particular rang me like a bell, and the energy of that moment has stayed with me ever since: 'Let us keep our eyes always fixed on the depths of our heart with an unceasing mindfulness of God.'[7]

As we read Mark's gospel we can have our eyes opened to the transforming kingdom that Jesus calls us to be part of. Like Jesus, we can enter into a spiritual relationship with God our Father through baptism, where we see heaven opened, the Spirit indwells us and we hear God's affirming words to us (Mark 1:9–11).

At work in all our relationships is the cross and resurrection of Jesus, 'For even the Son of Man did not come to be served, but to serve, and to give his life as a ransom for many' (Mark 10:45). This is where the hard and dirty work of the kingdom takes place.

This verse also tells us about the primary distortion within all our relationships – that of slavery, from which Jesus needs to ransom us. But we are also shown that we are blind and deaf to the beauty of the kingdom.

We need to learn to move in real relationship with God, with others and with the world. Jesus points out unreality and leads people towards the real throughout the gospel.

---

[7] Quoted in Olivier Clement, *The Roots of Christian Mysticism* (London: New City, 2002) p.204.

Throughout the gospel we also see the healing ministry of the kingdom, repairing us, our relationships and the beginning of all things being made new. As well as looking at Mark's theology of discipleship and especially watchfulness, we will also look at perspectives on these five archetypal relationships.

Another way of trying to describe what happens when we become more aware and attentive is to describe it as moving from doing to being. As I put myself in the place of silence and solitude as well as community, I found I moved from worry to peace. I found I was more in tune with the goodness of God at work in me and around me. I found a place of inner freedom. I believe this place is accessible to all of us – although we are not always aware that we are living on autopilot, driven by hidden fears and avoiding real relationship with God and others.

Before we move on to the practice of mindfully reading a chapter each day for 40 days, I want to outline a Christian perspective on mindfulness, beginning with attention and awareness.

A Christian perspective on awareness, attention and mindfulness

Today, as a parent, you might be praying for your child's ability to concentrate as they take another exam. On Boxing Day 2004 Tilly Smith, a 10-year-old British girl, saved 100 tourists on a Thai beach because she noticed that the waves were receding. She remembered her geography lessons and told her mum that the beach was about to be struck by a tsunami. I wonder why she paid attention in that particular lesson with her geography teacher, Andrew Kearney?

Two thousand years ago a centurion paid attention to the present moment, and as he saw how Jesus died he said, 'Surely this man was the Son of God!' (Mark 15:39)

At the birth of Jesus was a host of unimportant people who watched, waited and paid attention, as well as some important ones: the shepherds, the magi, Simeon and Anna, and Mary, who pondered and treasured all these things ('pondered' and 'treasured' are words about attention and awareness).

How about you?

Being able to sustain one's attention is generally considered to be a good thing. I guess we might think of it as an element in concentration. Whatever we are involved in, we need to be able to sustain our attention. In the Christian world, when we listen to a sermon it is an exercise in sustaining our attention. As our minds wander during the sermon it is an opportunity to practise switching our attention back to what the preacher is saying. We may catch ourselves telling an elaborate story in our head about something completely unconnected to the sermon, ruminating in a way that takes our attention away for many minutes.

Within the Bible there is an implicit theology of attention and awareness. Jesus goes off very early in the morning to a solitary place to pray, which is an act of sustained attention (Mark 1:35). Peter and the disciples hunt Him down and interrupt Him, trying to distract Him with what the crowd wants. Jesus switches His (and their) attention back to what really matters and says, 'Let us go somewhere else – to the nearby villages – so that I can preach there also. That is why I have come' (Mark 1:38).

Peter and the others were swept away by the stream of thoughts and feelings prompted by the crowds – perhaps thoughts of greatness and success. Jesus wasn't swept away by these elaborative and ruminative secondary processes that we all have and identify with.

29

Paul teaches us that we need to catch our afflictive thoughts and feelings early: 'In your anger do not sin' (Ephesians 4:26). Paul also talks about how we are stuck in automatic behaviours of sin: 'I do not understand what I do. For what I want to do I do not do, but what I hate I do' (Romans 7:15).

Jesus doesn't avoid the painful reality that awaits Him in Jerusalem. Three times in Mark's gospel He tells the disciples about how He must suffer many things, including rejection and death (Mark 8:31; 9:31; 10:33–34). The disciples are guilty of experiential avoidance, and cannot face that reality, with Peter even rebuking Jesus for talking about His death (Mark 8:32). Jesus accepts what they cannot accept – reality.

Jesus asks us to enter into a process of investigative awareness of what is going on in our hearts and minds: 'Why do you look at the speck of sawdust in your brother's eye and pay no attention to the plank in your own eye?' (Matthew 7:3). There is an ever-changing flow of thoughts and feelings within us; 'For from within, out of men's hearts, come evil thoughts' (Mark 7:21).

Diadochus of Photike talks about the same investigative awareness with God, where we are called to 'track' the 'footprints of the Invisible One.' [8]

Jesus asks us to discriminate between the things of God and the things of men (Mark 8:33). These moments, or states of awareness, are neither automatic nor automatically sustainable. Peter's acknowledgement of Jesus as the Christ is followed by his lack of understanding about why Jesus had to die upon a cross (Mark 8:29–33).

Part of the self-regulation of attention is the ability to switch our attention. Even when we are trying to sustain our

---

[8] Diadochus of Photike, *Following the Footsteps of the Invisible: The Complete Works of Diadochus of Photike,* Introduction, Translation and Notes by Cliff Ermatinger (Collegeville, Minnesota: Liturgical Press, 2010) p.69.

attention, our minds will wander, and so we will have to switch back to whatever it is we are concentrating on or attending to.

So whether it is school, college, home, work, relationships or the process of Christlike transformation, we all need to be able to regulate our attention, to sustain it and to switch it back and forth. It also means not becoming caught up in ruminative and elaborative patterns of thought that take our attention away from our object of focus. We all know how a train of thought can suddenly take us miles away from where we want to be. My wife very quickly spots when I am with her in body but not in spirit, as the saying goes. Children also notice this, and might hold your face in their hands and turn it towards them in order to be sure of your full attention.

At a theoretical level, these skills could be categorised as 'metacognitive' – that is, knowledge about and regulation of one's learning processes.

These terms – sustained attention, switching attention, self-regulation of attention, being in the present moment, elaborative and secondary processes, rumination, experiential avoidance, acceptance, intentional investigative awareness – are all terms and insights from the world of cognitive psychology. As Christians I think we can agree that they are good and God-given capacities within our minds that we should want to encourage and cultivate. They are also the first part of a proposed operational definition of mindfulness from a team of researchers.[9] Mindfulness as a mode of awareness that is a universal human capacity needs to be distinguished from the meditative, or mindful awareness practices, that evoke it.

---

[9] S. R. Bishop et al., 'Mindfulness: A Proposed Operational Definition' (2004). *Clinical Psychology: Science and Practice, 11* (230-241).

Often Christians only view mindfulness from one side – the Buddhist roots of many of the meditative or mindful awareness practices – and dismiss the idea of mindfulness. Approaching it from the point of view of cognitive psychology makes it more difficult to automatically dismiss. Of course, it is important to ask questions about the significance of the influence of these Buddhist roots on the development of mindfulness within Western psychology.[10]

If we approach mindfulness from this angle of regulated attention then there is a very strong case for it as a universal human capacity, a mode of awareness that is accessible to all. Its presence in many different religious traditions would suggest that it is a universal human capacity, and that there are different mindful awareness practices that can evoke it. If we look at the regulated attention practised by artists, poets and carpenters, for example, we can build an even stronger case for this hypothesis.

As Christians, we need to ask difficult questions of mindfulness, but we also have to approach it with a 360-degree focus. There is a Christian theology of mindfulness, and there are Christian mindful awareness practices (*Lectio Divina*, the Jesus Prayer, meditation, stillness, contemplation). We need to develop new forms of mindful awareness practices that include our body, our breath, and the ordinary weave of life around us.

Jesus commands watchfulness and mindfulness: 'What I say to you, I say to everyone: "Watch!"' (Jesus of Nazareth, Mark 13:37).

Sometime around AD 700 a Latin Gospel book now known as *The Lindisfarne Gospels* was made by Eadfrith, Bishop of

---

[10] If you would like to read more about this definition, see http://www.mindandsoul.info/Articles/339737/Mind_and_Soul/Resources/Articles/Mindfulness/A_Christian_perspective.aspx (accessed 21 January 2014).

Lindisfarne, probably over a ten-year period. Eadfrith took Jesus' command seriously, and the book was a work of sustained attention, a meditation of slow making. It is one of the wonders of the world. Such is the power of the Word and the Spirit working together with our awareness and attention. Christian mind*Full*ness is awareness of the presence of God at work within our own God-given capacities for attention and awareness.

We might ask the question, how can mindfulness be secular, Buddhist and Christian?

How can mindfulness be secular, Buddhist and Christian?

Firstly, mindfulness can be used in different settings because it is a universal human capacity for awareness and attention in the present moment It must be distinguished from the meditative or mindful awareness practices that lead to this mode of awareness.

The centre of gravity of attention and awareness was discovered very early on by all the major faith traditions. This emphasis on attention and awareness has a historical presence in Judaism and Christianity, as well as Buddhism. In secular psychology there has also been a long focus on awareness and attention and the regulation of emotions. In other words, people came across the capacity for mindfulness within different contexts; originally these contexts were religious. The other key idea, then, is to understand the context.

In counselling there is an important emphasis on client autonomy, respecting a person's worldview, experience and ethical values. That means boundaries are important. What is the context in which the client lives? An atheist might want to engage with a purely secular mindfulness. This question of boundaries and client autonomy arises in mindfulness because it is a universal human capacity and therefore appears in different contexts. Its forms must be well defined and clearly articulated, although there is shared territory between the forms as well as distinctives.

The key question is, I guess: how do we ensure that secular mindfulness is secular, that Buddhist mindfulness is Buddhist and that Christian mindfulness is Christian, for those to whom it matters? For someone looking at life through a secular lens, for example.

The answer is that it can be set within different frameworks, what Kabat-Zinn, the pioneer of mindfulness within secular psychology, calls 'scaffolding'.[11] Buddhist mindfulness has its own scaffolding, the different therapies within psychological mindfulness have their own scaffoldings, and Christian mindfulness has its own set of scaffoldings.

What I have been trying to develop, through *A Book of Sparks: a Study in Christian MindFullness* and other writings, is a Christian scaffolding, drawing on biblical and historical roots for the development of mindfulness within the Christian tradition, as well as looking at the benefits of engaging with it today. Within this setting I believe it has spiritual as well as therapeutic benefits, because of the overlaps and shared territory, and because we are 'embodied' people. The evidence-based research within clinical psychology suggests that it would also be appropriate to point Christians, under the holistic guidance of doctors and therapists, to secular clinical mindfulness which might address 'specific' vulnerabilities they might be living with. Christians are not immune from the

---

[11] Quoted in Richard Burnett, 'Mindfulness in Schools: Learning Lessons from the Adults, Secular and Buddhist' (October 2009), p.29. Available at http://mindfulnessinschools.org/research/richard-burnett-ma-dissertation/ (accessed 4 February 2014).

universal and specific vulnerabilities that afflict all human beings.

Within this research I am keen to work collaboratively with other Christians who are interested in mindfulness, both psychologically and theologically.

Mindfulness with a Christian scaffolding

Mindfulness within the Christian perspective is about not forgetting the things of God but remembering them. We can say this for a number of reasons. The Buddhist Pali word *sati*, often translated 'mindfulness', has at its root 'remembering'. So does the New Testament Greek word *mneme*, which can be translated as 'being mindful'.

In Psalm 8:4 the psalmist says, 'What is man that you are mindful of him?' In the Greek Septuagint version the word used is *mimneske* – to be mindful of, to actively remember. There is a high level of personal involvement in the remembering – that is mindfulness, the involvement of our awareness and attention.

James points out the danger of forgetfulness and the importance of remembering:

> Anyone who listens to the word but does not do what it says is like a man who looks at his face in a mirror and, after looking at himself, goes away and immediately forgets what he looks like. But the man who looks intently into the perfect law that gives freedom, and continues to do this, not forgetting what he has heard, but doing it – he will be blessed in what he does.
> *James 1:23-25*

James is talking about actively remembering here.

Jesus also puts remembering at the heart of being a mindful disciple:

> Do you still not see or understand? Are your hearts hardened? Do you have eyes but fail to see, and ears but fail to hear? And don't you remember?
> *Mark 8:17-18*

The Greek word here is *mnemoneute* – to be mindful of, to enduringly remember.

Why is this important? It is important because it can be given a different scaffolding to support it, depending on your point of view. So mindfulness can be used in different settings because it is a universal human capacity for awareness and attention in the present moment and, as we have said, must be distinguished from the meditative or mindful awareness practices that lead to this mode of awareness.

So the question is, what might mindfulness look like with a Christian scaffolding? As I have argued above, the central part of that scaffolding is about remembering and avoiding forgetfulness.

The importance of remembering and fleeing forgetfulness is also a central idea in Christian Benedictine spirituality. That is the scaffolding in which I would like to place mindfulness for in this section. In particular there is an aware humility at work in Benedictine spirituality. For example, I came across this comment by Columba Stewart OSB in *Prayer and Community: The Benedictine Tradition*:

> One must 'flee forgetfulness and always be mindful of what God has commanded' (RB 7:10-11).[12]

---

[12] Columba Stewart OSB, *Prayer and Community: The Benedictine Tradition* (London: DLT, 1998) p.28.

He calls this 'mindfulness of the presence of God'.[13] So at the heart of the Christian scaffolding for mindfulness within a Benedictine understanding is an awareness of the presence of God and remembering to translate into action what God wants us to do.

Why have I chosen Benedictine spirituality as an example? Well, I have been called a 'Benedictine Baptist' by one of the monks at Worth Abbey, Father Patrick. I would agree with that. The central vows of a Benedictine way of life seem to me to be at the heart of what it means to live out the gospel in the kingdom of God, through prayer and community. The particular take on these vows I want to outline is a summary of how I try to live in the world – as a minister, a married man, a father and a friend, with the help of this wisdom. At the heart would be the realisation that to be an aware, attentive and mindful person is central to that calling.

The first vow is one of stability, and at the heart of this is the gospel idea of persevering. Jesus says in Mark's gospel, 'but he who stands firm to the end will be saved' (Mark 13:13). This is about staying with one community and one place, and that is what I am trying to do in my ministry. What it means as a piece of scaffolding on which to build our life is that we stop looking to other places or other people, or to a future time where we imagine the grass might be greener. We have to focus on the present moment, where we are now, which is a central idea of mindfulness – living in present-moment awareness.

Jesus tells us to have stability in our watchfulness, our attentiveness to the kingdom of God: 'What I say to you, I say to everyone: "Watch!"' (Mark 13:37).

The second key piece of scaffolding is the vow of *conversatio morum*, often translated as 'conversion of life'. Its meaning is much debated, but I am applying it in a particular way.

---

[13] Ibid., p.28.

Another way it can be translated is as fidelity to the monastic way of life. Thomas Merton, a Benedictine monk, says that Mark 8:34–38, which is about taking up one's cross and following Christ, is at the heart of this vow. It is about a life 'which renounces care according to the teaching of the Sermon on the Mount in order to fix all the love and attention of the heart on Christ alone.'[14]

For me, this vow is about fixing all my love, attention and awareness on Christ and mindfully following in His footsteps. I see it as fidelity to a mindfully Christian way of life. As one mindfulness expert apparently said, mindfulness itself is not difficult – it is remembering to be mindful that is difficult.

Then you might say, 'Yes, but what does that look like?' Here we come to the last vow – that of listening obedience. This is the final piece of scaffolding. Jesus tells us that the good soil in the parable of the sower in Mark 4:1–9 is the attentive listener. A key part of Christian mindfulness is to listen attentively to the Word of God and to the living Word, Christ Himself. What emerges in this is a new mind, the Greek word *metanoiete*, which is sometimes translated 'repentance' (Mark 1:15). We are to leave behind our old habitual ways of thinking that are shaped in the patterns of this world, and allow the strange newness of the kingdom to emerge.

What emerges is not habitual, rule-bound patterns of thought and behaviour but an inner freedom that swims in the dynamic love of God for the world and its peoples. Each small fresh experience of stability, of attentiveness, of awareness, of listening obedience, lays down the way of living that is life in all its fullness.

---

[14] Thomas Merton, *The Monastic Journey* (London: Sheldon Press, 1977) p.111.

Summary

One way to have a map that helps us negotiate the main steps of mindfulness is to talk about four main movements we are involved in.

In their book *Teaching Mindfulness – A Practical Guide for Clinicians and Educators*, Donald McCown, Diane Reibel and Marc S. Micozzi outline these four movements.[15]

The first movement which comes out of the focus on coming to our bodily and inner senses is discovering our embodiment.[16] This is a theme of *A Book of Sparks*. The second movement is how we cultivate our capacity to observe.[17] The third movement is 'towards acceptance.'[18] In acceptance we face the full reality of our thoughts, feelings and sensations. The final movement is that involving a growth in compassion, towards the self and to others.[19]

When I was a child and at boarding school I would fly home in the holidays with an airline called the British Overseas Airways Corporation (BOAC). I have used these initials in a mnemonic to help us remember these four movements (changing them slightly) – because they help us to learn to fly!

- **B** – stands for the body, and reclaiming our body through our mindful awareness practices.

---

[15] Donald McCown, Diane Reibel, Marc S. Micozzi, *Teaching Mindfulness: A Practical Guide for Clinicians and Educators* New York: Springer, 2010.

[16] Ibid., p.168.

[17] Ibid., p. 175.

[18] Ibid., p.179.

[19] Ibid., p.185.

- **O** – stands for our ability to observe our thoughts, feelings and bodily sensations, moving out of living on autopilot.

- **A** – I use 'A' for awareness, and our ability to focus our attention as well as open up our awareness to all of the reality we experience. I have moved the important idea of acceptance as part of the move towards compassion.

- **C** – stands for the movement towards compassion, towards our own self, others, the world and God. In this compassionate attitude we accept the full reality of our internal thoughts, feelings and sensations non-judgementally.

Week One

Introduction

What I am about to outline is the cognitive pattern of being mindful that is distinctively Christian, but overlaps with secular mindfulness theory and practice.

One of the key verses in the Bible is Romans 12:2, 'Do not conform any longer to the pattern of this world, but be transformed by the renewing of your mind.' We need to watch for the patterns of this world that we have been formed into. For example, this week we will look at the idea that we have been formed by society to have an 'empty self'. This cognitive pattern of being mindful in a way that is distinctively Christian will run like a refrain throughout the book, so that it dwells in you richly.

In Mark's gospel, Jesus has an equally radical plan when He calls people to repent (Mark 1:15). The Greek word *metanoeite* literally means 'change of mind,' but not just changing your mind about what you are going to eat for supper. Jesus' demand for radical discipleship is actually a call for a new mind.

We are transformed through the twin tracks of God's living Word and the powerful work of the Holy Spirit. There are some key practices we need to follow in order to enable that transforming work. These include *Lectio Divina* – a slow spiritual reading of Scripture which allows the Holy Spirit to speak to us. At one time every Christian used to pray in this way. There are other important contemplative practices to try out which help us to begin this journey of increased awareness, including the use of prayer words and the memorisation of key verses of Scripture.

Our prayer needs to be the prayer of the psalmist, 'Test me, O Lord, and try me, examine my heart and my mind; for your love is ever before me' (Psalm 26:2–3). Like the psalmist, we need to open ourselves up to God to enable this examination.

One of the central disciplines within watchfulness that we need to learn comes out of another central verse, about the transformation of our hearts and minds: as the Apostle Paul says, 'we take captive every thought to make it obedient to Christ' (2 Corinthians 10:5).

How we do this is more difficult than knowing it to be true. We often live on autopilot in our thinking and feeling lives. Ask yourself what it says about your mind that you could take your own thoughts captive. Take some time before reading on.

One of the things it means is that we can observe our thoughts; we have an observing self within. This biblical verse also relativises our thoughts: we often think they are a perfect reflection of reality, but more often they are shaped in the patterns of this world – whether patterns of anxiety, anger or narcissism.

The way to take our thoughts captive is to disarm them. That's Christ's method, as with disarming the 'powers and authorities' (Colossians 2:15). Certain thoughts and thought patterns become like 'powers and authorities' in our lives. We disarm them by relativising them – they are not facts; they are thoughts that we can observe.

We make our thoughts obedient to Christ by treating them much as Jesus treated people, with one proviso: we remember they are not real. They are like clouds in the sky, not bricks in a wall. We notice them with compassion and love, accept them for what they are, and then let them go, send them on their way saying, 'Go and sin no more.' In this way they lose their power and authority over us and can no longer afflict us or, if they are sinful thoughts, lead us to sin.

As you read this book each day, keep a journal. Try to catch your thoughts – negative ones, automatic ones or creative ones that you might miss. Observe your thoughts each day. Which ones turn into a dramatic soap opera around particular themes of hurt, or anger? Paradoxically we take them captive by noticing them and then letting them go, as if each thought is a leaf on a stream.

As you go through Mark's gospel, read it as a whole, read the chapters designated each week, and read passages that speak to you slowly and over again, in the form of *Lectio Divina*. This is mindful reading.

Mnemonics are often used in mindfulness training and I have adapted one of them because the word 'coal' has deep Christian resonance. Use the mnemonic COAL for the process of reading slowly. Think of the words you are reading as the living coal of God's Word. Ask the Holy Spirit to breathe on the words and fan them into flame. Breathe on them with the breath of your attention.

- **C** – stands for 'curiosity'. Be passionately and dangerously inquisitive about what you are reading and rereading. In our curiosity we stay with the passage, reading it slowly. We leave a gap of silence between each slow reading.

- **O** – stands for 'openness'. Be completely open to what God might be saying to you in a whisper, in a hint, in a riddle. It is in the slow reading and in the gap that we are opening ourselves up, and allowing ourselves to be opened up by the Holy Spirit.

- **A** – stands for 'attentiveness'. Thoughts and feelings, other stories will come into your mind and distract you.

Keep coming back to the passage you are reading. In this way you strengthen your ability to be attentive. What does God want you to do today? In this in-between place of the living Word of God, the Holy Spirit links our world to God's world. The Word links us to the person and presence of God. Try to find just the one thing God wants you to do this day – the one thing to pray for.

- L – stands for 'live it out'. This is not just about doing, but about staying in the place of being, which is the heart of contemplation. Come back to the Word during the day. Perhaps memorise one verse.

The final step in the process is to take the word 'coal' to represent the burning, purifying presence of God (Isaiah 6:6) and just rest in that presence in a place of contemplative awareness that is beyond words.

Remember, each week we are looking at the five key relationships in which our lives play out their story:

- The spiritual relationship with God the Father, others and the world – the relationship that inhabits all others.

- Our need to become real and authentic, to be in person-to-person relationships where we treat no one or no thing as 'IT' but only as 'THOU'.

- Where we face the fact that we need to work at all our relationships, and have a working relationship with all things.

- Where we realise that we enter into distorted relationships and people have a distorted view of us.

- Finally we need to realise that we are all wounded, and need to enter into repairing relationships, as well as being a repairer of relationships.

In terms of spiritual disciplines, I believe the following put us in the place for spiritual transformation:

- Reading Mark's gospel as a whole.

- *Lectio Divina* as a way of memorising Scripture and hearing the voice of God. By staying with one passage all week we go deep into the living Word, instead of a shallow multiplicity of skimming over many passages.

- The Jesus Prayer as a way into the presence of God.

- Memorising Scripture.

- Deep looking at the wisdom and goodness imbedded in God's world, His many-sided wisdom which develops our discernment.

As we read each day, I would encourage you to read slowly, and mind*Fully*; the very process of this type of reading can bring us into a place of awareness and attentiveness, tuning us into God, our self, and the world. We begin to see straight and true, something that Mark tells us in his gospel we do not do without God's transforming power.

This is not something we are used to, and it is something that we can easily and automatically dismiss. Let me say a bit more about mindful reading.

I was born in Kenya and we didn't have a TV or computers or any other technical distractions. My mum taught me to read at the age of three, and it is one of the greatest gifts I have been given. I learnt to lose myself in books. I learnt to speed-read. I learnt to read selectively for academic study. But the most difficult form of reading, and perhaps the most important, is to read mindfully.

Mindful reading is different. One way I learnt to do this – and I am still learning – was through the slow prayerful reading of sacred text that is *Lectio Divina*. This slow form of reading is repetitive, lovingly repetitive. It is meditative and contemplative.

I also learnt a lot about reading mindfully, and was inspired to read other books in this way by Miriam Darlington's lyrical *Otter Country*.[20] We can read other texts that inspire mindful reading; it doesn't have to be Scripture.

I take *Otter Country* with me whenever I lead a retreat, a listening day or a seminar, and I read sections to illustrate mindful reading and mindful attentiveness through observing the natural world.

One of the main practices of *A Book of Sparks: A Study in Christian Mind*Full*ness* is mindful reading. This is not as easy as it sounds, mainly because we are trained to read in another way. I came across a brilliant explanation of mindful or contemplative reading in a book about training mindfulness teachers. This is what they say:

> Rather than aggressively reading to have knowledge and gain 'truth,' participants learn a method which is a *being with,* not a *doing of* the text – an embodied, not a cognitive encounter.[21]

We are so used to aggressively reading as an act of doing of or to the text, we do not know how to be with the text, especially text that does not immediately surrender its meaning.

Mindfulness-Based Cognitive Therapy (MBCT) talks about learning to shift from the doing mode of mind to the being mode of mind. We are culturally conditioned in particular to inhabit the doing mode of mind. Our aggressive reading of texts reflects this. The shift to being happens through mindful

---

[20] Miriam Darlington, *Otter Country* (London: Granta, 2012).
[21] Donald McCown, Diane Reibel & Marc S. Micozzi, *Teaching Mindfulness*, p.160.

awareness practices, meditative practices. One such practice, I believe, is mindful reading.

There is great power in the repetition of such practices, in establishing a rhythm each day where we slow down and give time to God.

Day 1: The kingdom of making new

Read Mark 1
Memorise Mark 1:35

BEGINNING. That's how Mark's gospel starts, with the single Greek word *arche*. This is a word of echoes and resonances. In the Greek version of the Old Testament, the Septuagint, the same word launches the book of Genesis: 'In the beginning...'

The coming of Jesus is about making things new, bigger than the first creation. Another way of saying this is that 'the kingdom of God is near' (Mark 1:15). When the moon is closest to the earth – the peligree moon – it affects the tides. When the kingdom is near it affects the tides of history, time and all created things.

It is no coincidence that at the beginning of the gospel of Mark Jesus goes off to a solitary place, very early in the morning, to pray (Mark 1:35). If we want to begin in the new beginnings of the kingdom, we need to start the day in a solitary place and pray. When we do that we step into the gravitational pull of the kingdom of making new.

When Simon and the other followers come looking for Him, in the original language of the gospel, they literally 'hunt' Him down. There are many other distractions in our lives that will hunt us down when we try to pray. One of the riddles set at the beginning of Mark is that if we want to be available to others, we need to make ourselves radically unavailable. Mark's gospel is full of riddles, mysteries, veiled ambiguities, paradoxes, echoes and resonances from elsewhere in Scripture. Like good poetry it does not surrender its meanings easily; we have to search for them hungrily.

We can all too easily miss the point. One of the earliest echoes is about suffering. It is just a whisper at the beginning of the book. When Jesus is baptised, His Father in heaven says, 'You are my Son, whom I love; with you I am well pleased' (Mark 1:11). In the Greek this is emphatic: 'My son the beloved' – and a direct echo of the phrase in the Greek version of the Old Testament in Genesis 22:2 – the story of Isaac, another beloved son who is to be sacrificed, but for whom in the end a replacement is found. The story ends in a different way for Jesus of Nazareth.

One of the profoundest themes in the gospel is the stark presentation of how the disciples (and by implication we) are painfully dis-located from understanding Jesus and the kingdom; how complex a task it is to locate that place of understanding within; and how long it takes to re-locate to the place where the kingdom is near. Even after numerous miracles, Jesus' lament to His disciples in Mark 8:17 is, 'Do you still not see or understand?' In other words, our thoughts are not an accurate readout of reality. Mark's gospel asks us to decentre from our thoughts and examine them, and so does mindfulness.

Our central task is to locate that place of understanding and awareness within. Finding that place is a gift from God, but we are also called to play our part – whether it is by putting ourselves in the place of stillness and solitude, allowing the Word to indwell us, or sailing close to the wind of the Spirit.

Our culture has given us double-glazed eyes and selective hearing. We need Mark's gospel to grasp the pain of our dis-location, and snap our understanding back into place.

If we are to notice the echoes and resonances, comprehend the riddles, then we need the attentiveness and awareness that comes with Jesus' command to be watchful (Mark 13:37).

Stay with Mark 1:35–39 this week, with the slow reading of *Lectio Divina*. As you do this, hopefully by the end of the week you will be close to having memorised it. We want this to be a passage that comes back to you through the work of the Holy

Spirit, reminding you to find that place within and that space in the world to pray.

Day 2: The Empty Self – working on our self-awareness

As Christians we believe that we have a relational God who lives in a community of love – Father, Son and Holy Spirit. As human beings we are made in God's image, which makes us relational creatures. It is interesting that evolutionary psychologists have also discovered that we are relational creatures. Mindfulness within psychology is also about our ability to relate to others in an aware and attentive way – we have a social brain.

The main condition we have to wrestle with is that we are empty. We will not be undone by empty talk, or being empty-handed in the current consumer economy, but by our empty selves.

Some philosophers and psychologists, Christian and otherwise, characterise the post-war self as an empty one. We need a D-Day of the soul, where God's love invades us and occupies the territory we currently fill with consumer goods, unneeded food, artificial stimulants and busyness. Obesity is an increasingly recognised national problem. In addition, there are many who embody emptiness by refusing food.

Jesus warned of the danger of emptiness, and more profoundly than just running on empty. In the parable of the Ten Virgins, the foolish ones are those with the empty lamps, who have no interior life (Matthew 25:8). In Matthew 12 the evil spirit which comes out of a man returns with seven others worse than itself to fill the empty soul (verses 43–45). Our inner emptiness is implied when the Bible affirms the importance of being filled by the Holy Spirit (Acts 2:4).

The way out of an economic crisis, according to some, is for us, the consumers, to spend our way out of trouble. Our government, as with others in the West, constructed a post-war economy based on the production of far more consumer goods than required to fuel economic growth. This was fanned by the growth in easy credit and the rise of an advertising industry proficient in psychological manipulation. Every advert tells us that we are empty unless we fill ourselves with their product.

There is a spiritual solution. Instead of mindlessly existing as vacuum cleaners sucking up all the consumer items we can, attempting and failing to fill our emptiness, we can cultivate the watchfulness that Jesus commends (Mark 13:37).

Not many modern books on prayer stress the importance of cultivating this attention, but in the *Philokalia* – a collection of Christian texts written between the fourth and the fifteenth centuries – a state of watchfulness is considered the hallmark of sanctity.[22]

Lacking this awakened attention, we are seemingly unaware of this construct of our time, the empty self – which afflicts Christians as much as it does any secular person.

Ray Mears, the survival expert, talks about a vanishing world of wilderness, wisdom and bushcraft. The watchfulness Jesus teaches us is bushcraft of the soul.

The minimum night watch in biblical times was three hours. If you failed to stay attentive you could be beaten and have your clothes set on fire. This adds poignancy to Jesus' lament to Peter, 'Could you not keep watch for one hour?' (Mark 14:37). The average attention span today is assessed at between seven and 11 minutes, although it can be measured in seconds for internet browsing.

The question to ask ourselves is, 'With what am I filling my empty self?'

---

[22] G. E. H. Palmer, P. Sherrard & K. Ware (Eds.), *The Philokalia* (London: Faber & Faber, 1979).

I know for myself that not owning my own house has shown me how I would long to fill my inner emptiness with home ownership. A few years ago, getting rid of my car showed me how much I filled my emptiness with the status and freedom of car ownership.

In our society these things have ceased to be icons of God's grace and have become idols that replace the space God is to fill within us. Contemplate taking them away and suddenly the presence of God is intensified in us.

If we seek first the kingdom of God, if the inexhaustible tongue of fire that is the Holy Spirit rests on us, we can resist the siren call of consumerism to fill our empty selves. Try it! Unlike the adverts, it works.

The riddle and the paradox of truth within the idea of an empty self is that we are in pain and incomplete, because we have an empty space within us where God should be. We are filling that space with the wrong things.

Day 3: *Lectio Divina* and spiritual awareness

I have spent a number of three-day retreats at Worth Abbey in Sussex, where BBC TV's *The Monastery* series was filmed. My introduction to the series that was watched by three million viewers and broadcast in 2005 was the book *Finding Sanctuary*,[23] written by Abbott Christopher Jamison in response to the interest generated by the programme.

The book inspired me to obtain copies of *The Monastery* programmes to watch in our men's house group. The impact on the group was profound.

For those who haven't seen the series, *The Monastery* involved five very modern men living the Benedictine monastic life for 40 days and 40 nights. We watched with open mouths as these five men struggled to live in community and as the monks supported them patiently and lovingly. But the monks also had deep insight into the issues pulling each of the participants down, and were able to challenge the men in a way that went below their defences.

The other thing that impressed us was the Christlikeness of the monks, and the power of the monastic way of life, with its emphasis on silence, solitude and regular patterns of prayer, as well as living in community.

The men in our group were deeply challenged by the shallowness of their own spiritual lives and expressed a desire to go on some sort of retreat, where this pattern of living and praying could be experienced. My own prayer life has blown hot and cold and been stuck on many occasions, and so I found myself immersed in the monastic life for three days.

---

[23] Abbot Christopher Jamison, *Finding Sanctuary* (London: Phoenix, 2006).

I remember being very struck by peace activist Norman Kember's comments when he returned from captivity in Iraq, that his spirituality hadn't prepared him for captivity. I talk to many folk who say their spirituality hasn't prepared them for old age.

So what is this spirituality we need to work on? In many cases it has become about activity – doing things, being busy.

A disciple of Christ, says Dallas Willard, is someone transformed into 'the goodness and power seen in Jesus.[24] Activities don't make us Christlike, only the practice of personal spiritual disciplines.

The two Benedictine monks who guided the Finding Sanctuary retreat – Father Rod and Father Patrick – were Catholic priests, immersed in Word and Spirit. There is a family resemblance which means in Christ I was able to trust them and learn from them.

We arrived on the Friday night and spent the Saturday following their offices of prayer, singing at least 15 psalms as well as other passages of Scripture. In a four-week cycle the monks sing most of the psalms.

If our spirituality is about being people of the Book, we need to learn from this tradition where Scripture is simply allowed to speak for itself – a communion with the Word rather than just drily extracting a message.

This communion with the Word is further enhanced by the monks through the spiritual discipline of *Lectio Divina* – a slow, contemplative reading of Scripture. One of the reasons I went to Worth Abbey was to help develop that discipline for myself, a discipline I first came across in Michael Quicke's excellent book *360-Degree Preaching*.[25]

---

[24] Dallas Willard, *Renovation of the Heart* (Leicester: IVP, 2002) p.20.
[25] Michael Quicke, *360-Degree Preaching* (Grand Rapids Michigan: Baker Academic, 2003).

Another aspect of this spirituality I want to develop is a passion – a warm heart, not just an intellectual faith. One of the attested fruits of the Jesus Prayer developed by the Desert Fathers, forerunners of the monastic movements, is its power to set hearts on fire, through the repetition in a reverential way of the name of Jesus. Both the Benedictine rhythm of praying five times a day and the Jesus Prayer are responses to the biblical command to pray continually (1 Thessalonians 5:17).

Yet another fundamental aspect of the spirituality I would like to develop is the desire to witness and evangelise. Are we too busy to develop Christlikeness? And yet Christlikeness has a contagious beauty which draws people to us.

I want to emphasise the power of these contemplative disciplines to change anybody's life. Once again at Worth Abbey I was helped by being in relationship with others. These are people of difference, from a different denomination, but people with wisdom and love.

These disciplines develop the spiritual awareness that Jesus commends, and also influence our ability to relate well in all our relationships. These repetitive spiritual practices also begin to change our neuro-plastic brains for the better. Andrew Newberg, an American neuroscientist, says, 'meditating on any form of love, including God's love, appears to strengthen the same neurological circuits that allow us to feel compassion toward others.'[26] A lot more evidence is now available about how meditative or mindful awareness practices change the structure and activity of our brains for the better.

---

[26] A. Newberg, & M. R. Waldman, *How God Changes Your Brain* (New York: Ballantine, 2010) p.53.

Day 4: A real relationship with our creativity

One of my favourite paintings at the moment is *The Mystical Boat* by the French Symbolist Odilon Redon. It speaks to my deep self, that part of me that is made in the image of God. It resonated with great power because for a period of months I drew sailing boats with me in them.

Since Noah's Ark, boats have been a powerful sacred symbol. When they emerge in our consciousness it is worth looking at the reasons. There is a frustrated Argonaut in each one of us, and a Golden Fleece we need to seek.

But we have to journey on our own. One of the highways of the sea that lead us to God is the awareness that for much of the journey we are alone and responsible alone.

Often the Golden Fleece is only found in darkness. We usually flee from that darkness rather than seek it out.

I started drawing small sailing boats with me in them after reading Ursula Le Guin's *A Wizard of Earthsea*. Written in the 1960s for children, it is a book that can lead anyone to their deeper self. The hero, Ged, who is everyman or everywoman, lets loose a shadow in the world that hunts him and from which he flees.

The turning point of the book is when Ged receives a word of life from a wise old man, that he must turn around and hunt the shadow – 'the hunted must become the hunter'. He makes a small boat with a sail and sets out on the sea, and the shadow flees from him, as it begins to take on his likeness.

We all have a shadow side that we deny, but which needs to be reintegrated. *The Mystical Boat* depicts the journey after that hardest work has been done. When Jesus stands on the beach in John 21 and says to Peter, 'Simon son of John, do you truly love me more than these?' Simon Peter is forced to face the shadow of his betrayal. His words of love to Jesus in response now include the painfully acknowledged dark thread of betrayal as well as the deep blue of faithfulness to follow.

In religious life we are all prone to creating a shadow – the parts of ourselves we have repressed for fear of rejection or being judged. Another way of looking at it is to say Christians often have a front-stage that conforms to the perceived morality of their community, and a back-stage where their hidden life is. Hidden addictions like alcohol, drugs or pornography are shadows, work on which has not yet been done.

I realised I needed to launch a symbolic boat and sail in it to track down my shadow, with the fear of rejection lurking at the heart of it. Only then can we begin to move on from Paul's cry, and all of our cries, 'For what I want to do I do not do, but what I hate I do' (Romans 7:15). Only then does the cry, 'I do not understand what I do' become a cry of understanding and metamorphosis rather than a cry of despair. Facing our shadow is the opposite of what psychological mindfulness calls 'experiential avoidance' – where we try to run away from aspects of our internal experience we find intolerable – especially negative feelings and thoughts.

We can use the language of 'sin' and 'old self' but our task is to find new words to say those things, words that resonate with people in our culture without watering down the meaning God intends.

And not all of our shadow is about sin. I have repressed creative aspects of myself like writing poetry or painting pictures to express what I feel because I have been told these things are not 'real'. How many of us have these parts of our selves waiting to be released?

On another retreat at Worth Abbey I felt I had to paint a second picture of me in a sailing boat, but this time in an embrace of reconciliation. The embrace was inspired by a sculpture at Coventry Cathedral, a duplicate of which is in the

Peace Garden in Hiroshima, Japan. This picture, too, is one of hope, a picture of now or a picture of the future. The embrace could be with my shadow, someone I love, or God, or all of them.

It was after I had painted my two paintings – hunting my shadow, and the embrace of reconciliation – that I came across *The Mystical Boat*. I was suddenly filled with tremendous hope that wholeness, reintegration and reconciliation were possible and could be the next painting representing my journey towards God. I suddenly had insight into what my paintings might mean for me.

What I want to share in this personal story is that God speaks to us in many different kinds of ways. He is the creative Creator and utilises our creativity in His dialogue with us.

Are there aspects of your own creativity that you are repressing?

Day 5: The distortion of narcissism

If ego is the poison of leadership, then narcissism is the primary ingredient of that poison. Narcissism is a post-modern psychological term with ancient roots that should have real interest for churches and leaders. It is also a real problem for ordinary people in the workplace who have a narcissistic boss. It is a classic factor that distorts relationships between people.

Clinical Professor of Leadership Development Manfred Kets de Vries says that on the continuum of human behaviour there is healthy narcissism and unhealthy narcissism – what he calls reactive narcissism.[27]

According to *The Diagnostic and Statistical Manual of the Mental Disorders* (DSM-IV-TR),[28] reactive narcissism, which is on the increase amongst leaders, is characterised by a pervasive pattern of grandiosity, need for admiration and a lack of empathy. Causing great damage in organisations, danger signals of reactive narcissism include:

- a grandiose sense of self-importance

- having fantasies of unlimited success and power

- a belief that he (usually) is special and unique and should only associate with other high-status people

- requiring excessive admiration

- having a sense of entitlement and a belief that others should automatically comply with his expectations

---

[27] Manfred Kets de Vries, *The Leader on the Couch* (Chichester: John Wiley & Sons Ltd, 2006) p.29.

[28] Quick Reference to *The Diagnostic and Statistical Manual of the Mental Disorders* (DSM-IV-TR) (Washington DC: APA, 2000) p.294.

- being interpersonally exploitative
- lacking empathy
- being envious of others and believing that others are envious of him
- showing arrogant and haughty attitudes

There are also a host of recognisable techniques for acquiring position and power, usually covertly, that go with these patterns of behaviour.

One of the theological challenges is that in their extreme form, personality disorders, including narcissism, appear to be almost untreatable from a psychological perspective. One of the main ethical challenges is how to manage a narcissist who is trying to gain power covertly, without utilising the same underhand and behind-the-scenes tactics.

We probably live in the most narcissistic culture of all time, so narcissism as a problem is only going to increase, and not just among leaders.

Research including books on the subject of narcissism is burgeoning rapidly, with titles ranging from *Snakes in Suits: When Psychopaths Go to Work*,[29] to Manfred Kets de Vries' *The Leader on the Couch*.[30]

In another theological parallel, Jonathan Burnside, writing for The Jubilee Centre (a Christian social reform organisation), sees the modern secular society and its fascination with using power covertly as giving in 'to the same attitudes that are manifest in witchcraft'.[31] Cultic leaders might well be called

---

[29] Paul Babiak & Robert D. Hare, *Snakes in Suits: When Psychopaths Go to Work* (London: Harper, 2006).
[30] See earlier reference.
[31] Jonathan Burnside, 'Covert Power: Unmasking the World of Witchcraft', *Cambridge Papers* Vol. 19 No. 4 (2010) p.10.

'snakes in suits' in the light of the sinister sway they exercise power over others.

The key questions are, 'How do we spot reactive narcissism in ourselves and in others?' and 'How do we tackle it?'

One of the problems is the lack of awareness among leaders and followers about the whole area of narcissism. This is not only a lack of self-awareness but an inability to diagnose reactive narcissism when it manifests itself. From the perspective of mindfulness I would say that narcissists are often looking at their world from their thoughts, assuming that what they see is an exact replica of reality. The problem is that they are not living in reality. The antidote is shifting to look at their thoughts through mindful awareness practices, and in the mindful looking to realise that their thoughts are distorted.

Another problem is that narcissists are often good at impression management and hiding their real agenda and desire for power until they obtain a position of power. By then it is often too late and very difficult to remove the person from that position of power.

A further problem is that a reactive narcissist will not tolerate any criticism, with attack being their first form of defence. People soon learn to avoid criticising a narcissistic leader, even constructively, because of the aggressive counter-responses.

Within the church, a leader can of course say that God is behind him – and who can argue with God? When God is used to support an authoritarian, controlling and 'untouchable' ministry, then this is a 'red-flag' danger signal.

Part of the solution is to ensure that love as the heartbeat of Christian ministry is a challenging love that diagnoses the afflictive thoughts and worldly patterns of behaviour of our fallen minds.

It is ironic that searching our hearts (which is commended) lies next to the theme of secrecy (which is condemned) in the thematic index of the NIV Thematic Study Bible. 'Search me, O God, and know my heart,' says the psalmist (Psalm 139:23). Bringing the shadow side of leadership into the light of God is the next part of the story.

When we are narcissistic, and we are all on that spectrum, we replace the 'eco' of ecology with 'ego' and we damage the biosphere of all our relationships. We are often unaware of how culturally shaped we are in this direction. We need to become aware of it as a primary distortion in our lives and culture. The question then to ask is, 'What can we do to change?'

Day 6: Repairing our view of the body

As Christians we need to value the body much more. Paradoxically, the sex-saturated world in which we live is a sign that our culture does not value the body enough.

Sadly, many Christians do not value their bodies enough, trapped as they are in a view that spirit is good and body is bad. Manichaeus, who lived in the third century, was one of the first Christians to condemn the body and sexuality, seeing the material world as evil.

This error was condemned by the church as a heresy. However, Manichaeism seems to be alive and well in the contemporary church. One of the challenges of mindfulness within psychology is precisely the emphasis they have of living less in our heads and more in embodied reality. We need a new theology of the body which recognises it as the hinge of theology from the beginning to the end of the biblical story.

This would help redeem the image of the church in the whole area of the body and sexuality. It is seen as prudish, repressive and irrelevant by a world undergoing a profound sexual crisis. We may have help in this reconfiguring of the meaning of human embodiment from unlikely sources.

It is often on retreats that God gives me a new insight into something. On another three-day retreat at Worth Abbey, the Benedictine Catholic monastery, I had the opportunity to look at some teaching on the body by Pope John Paul II which became a major theme of his pontificate, especially focusing on sexuality and erotic desire.[32]

---

[32] Christopher West, *Theology of the Body for Beginners: A Basic Introduction to Pope John Paul II's Sexual Revolution* (West Chester, Pennsylvania: Ascension Press, 2004).

Why did God give us bodies in the beginning? Pope John Paul II argues that it is to make visible something of the invisible mystery of God. When we look forward to Christmas, when the Word of God became flesh, the body re-enters theology by the main door.

As embodied creatures, many of our deepest experiences involve the affirmation of our bodies, and the most painful involve the rejection of our bodies. At the age of six I was first sent to boarding school, experiencing it as a rejection. The loss of the visible embodied closeness of my family was traumatic.

The fear of rejection lies at the root of much of our inadequate relating – whether we keep our distance physically and emotionally, interpret relationships suspiciously or cling to others.

For me, God began to do a healing work when I realised my mother didn't intend sending me away as a rejection. This healing continued at my short stay at Worth Abbey early on a Sunday morning before the sun rose as I contemplated a crucifix hanging from the Abbey ceiling and read the words of Jesus: 'This is my body given for you' (Luke 22:19).

Other times in my life when someone had given their body for me suddenly came back to me, and almost for the first time I realised the profound significance of Jesus' words through the remembrance of these other profound givings.

My mother had given her body to me, housing me in her womb – letting her body be my home. The natural, spiritual and intense bond of breastfeeding is another archetypal event when a body is given for another.

My father once protected my sister and me by putting his body between us and a shoal of jellyfish when we were swimming in the sea. Another time he put his body in the way of an aggressive drunk to protect the two of us.

In marriage, there is great healing when we are fully seen by our loved one physically, emotionally and spiritually, and fully see another. As our bodies are given one to another in sexual union, one of the great existential truths is that we become 'one flesh' (Genesis 2:24). That is why there is great hurt in marriage when we give our bodies to others through so-called 'casual' affairs.

Again, help in this area is coming from an unlikely source. Dr David Schnarch is a clinical psychologist and marriage therapist who, although not a Christian, recognises the spiritual element to sexuality. His research and work with hundreds of couples shows that the best sex occurs between emotionally committed couples who choose to stay together and not to have other partners – because only in that context is it possible to know someone deeply.

In our post-modern disposable culture, bodies are given away too easily in what David Schnarch calls the mindless 'piece of meat' model of sex, disposed of too easily through abortion and euthanasia.[33]

Every year in November we remember those who have given their bodies in times of war in what is often called the ultimate sacrifice, that we might enjoy peace.

If as Christians we can present the true biblical theology of the body, we can encourage a culture of life rather than death. Our culture, with its emphasis on techniques and sensation in sex, has completely lost sight of what true intimacy is.

One of the mindful awareness practices within psychological mindfulness that I find helpful is the body scan.[34] Focusing your awareness on each part of the body, you open yourself to how you are feeling in your body. It is a neutral practice that anyone can do, regardless of their religious or otherwise background. It helps to still the noise

---

[33] David Schnarch, *Passionate Marriage* (New York/London: W. W. Norton & Co, 1997) p.79.
[34] www.franticworld.com/free-meditations-from-mindfulness/ (accessed 21 January 2014).

within and is a very human thing to do. Although it has psychological benefits, it can also be used as a preparation for a time of contemplation.

As a church, we need to reopen the main door and let the body back in to spirituality, and let spirituality back into the body.

Day 7: Remaking comes near

In the kingdom, the great primary energy of making and remaking comes near, its effects invisible, much like the pull of the moon on the oceans, real but invisible. Only the kingdom can save the planet. And yet we are called to be part of the kingdom as incredibly fragile beings. We can have moments of epiphany, and then go for years without seeing clearly.

Let's just summarise what we have said so far.

The goal of discipleship is laid out in Romans 12:2: 'Do not conform any longer to the pattern of this world, but be transformed by the renewing of your mind.'

How we begin to do this is laid out in 2 Corinthians 10:5: 'We demolish arguments and every pretension that sets itself up against the knowledge of God, and we take captive every thought to make it obedient to Christ.'

Of course, the most important question then is, 'Yes, but how?'

We begin with contemplation. Contemplation moves from saying prayers as a shopping list presented to God, to prayer where we are listening to God and are in His presence.

The problem is that we do not know what is in our own minds. We are not aware of our habitual thought patterns and so we do not know how to take them captive. The first truth is that our minds become fixed in habitual patterns, often sinful.

'Do not conform any longer to the pattern of this world...' (Romans 12:2).

The devil wants to fix us down, nail us down in our old fixed self. Paul says:

> You were taught, with regard to your former way of life, to put off your old self, which is being corrupted by its deceitful desires; to be made new in the

attitude of your minds; and to put on the new self, created to be like God in true righteousness and holiness.
Ephesians 4:22–24

That new self is a clear and present reality. Paul also says, 'So I say, live by the Spirit, and you will not gratify the desires of the sinful nature' (Galatians 5:16).

That is, we are to live in the present moment with the Spirit and we will access this new self. Mindfulness is present-moment awareness, and the Spirit helps us to be mindful of the new possibilities of the new self. This new self is not fixed but fluid with the wisdom of the Holy Spirit. How do we find our new self?

Jesus says in John 14 of the devil, 'He has no hold over me' (verse 30) or in the NKJV, 'He has nothing in Me.' The devil and sin have no hold on your new self; light is separated from darkness.

We access our new self by knowing the pattern of our mind, which we arrive at through contemplation – like *Lectio Divina* or the Jesus Prayer.

Wisdom talks about our fixed mind, but also about the mind of folly.

Our culture encourages us to gratify the desires of our sinful nature, to give in to our urges. These then become fixed habits. These urges come as waves, and the fluid Holy Spirit helps us to surf these urges without giving into them, until they die down.

The fluid Holy Spirit enables us to move out of our fixed mind and into a new wise mind where thought and feeling come together in listening obedience to God.

What you are then looking for is an awareness of God's presence arising at times in ordinary activity. What is this like? It's like colour being added to a black-and-white TV screen. Contemplative prayer brings us into the present moment.

God as a reality is always present, always in the present. That is where we will find Him. In your fixed patterns you will find you are often ruminating about the past or worrying about the future – yet you can change neither of these things. Letting these things go is part of being mindful or contemplative.

In Mark's gospel Jesus takes the ordinary visible things of this world – ears of corn, seeds, lamps, pigs, bread and fish – and points us to the invisible presence of God through them. This is something we will come back to later in the book.

The key thing we need to map is the pattern of our thoughts and feelings and the stories we wrap them up in. We need to realise that we are not our thoughts and feelings, that we are bigger than them. The Bible tells us that these thoughts and feelings are shaped in the patterns of this world (Romans 12:2): anxious, angry, competitive, acquisitive, fearful (Mark 8– 10). They are not an accurate readout of reality. But before we can let them go we need to know what they are for us.

Week Two

Day 8: Peter and a crisis experience

Read Mark 8:31–38

There is a theology of crisis within Mark's gospel, especially in the area of re-locating us as disciples into the place of seeing and hearing and of understanding. In these 40 days I don't want to tell you what to think, but to try and tease you into thinking for yourself. Keep a copy of Mark's gospel to hand each day, and this week trace the journey of Peter through the gospel.

One of the miracles of Mark's gospel is that it should be read and heard as a whole. I won't give you all the references that show us Peter's journey; you can track them down for yourself. But let's look at an early crisis of Peter's.

The characterisation of the disciples has perplexed scholars over a number of years now. They seem to suffer from a primal deafness, have shutters over their eyes and where Jesus calls them to listen, they seem able to hear only in the shallows of God's kingdom.

The first seven chapters of Mark's gospel are full of the dazzle of kingdom miracles. But that dazzle is not enough. There is a deeper, darker thread that needs to be sewn into the tapestry. From Mark 8:31 onwards, Jesus predicts His suffering and death. He is speaking openly here and not in riddles, and Peter takes Him aside and begins to rebuke Him.

'Out of my sight, Satan!' Jesus says (8:33), using a word that carries the force of an exorcism. Peter must be dis-located from his understanding. As you read chapter 8, write down what you think Jesus says true discipleship really is.

Mark's gospel is like a complex tree of meaning, intricate patterns of life working together to bring us revelation. But Jesus says there are only two ways of thinking. He says to Peter, as part of His rebuke, 'You do not have in mind the concerns of God, but merely human concerns' (8:33). Peter has followed but not understood.

This should puzzle us. We have to put human concerns behind us and re-locate our minds on the things of God. In our dis-location we follow the pattern of this world in the anxious saving of self, although in doing that we lose our true self (Mark 8:35). Jesus is asking us to be mindful of our thoughts, feelings and ruminative patterns. The 'merely human concerns' that we are caught up in are not as real as we think they are. The 'concerns of God' that Jesus asks us to be mindful of are more real than we think they are.

This riddle is worth memorising and then meditating on. What does it mean for me? What does it mean for you? The parables and riddles of Jesus tease us into awareness. They are one of His spiritual tools for helping us to be mindful and aware.

In our culture we desire to save ourselves because we have absorbed the narcissism of our world. Lucifer fell through the sin of narcissism, a form of pride. In our minds we become 'somebody' because we have a certain car, or house, or job, or wear certain clothes. In this way we believe we are saving ourselves. Paradoxically, by following the lure of the advertising world we become part of the herd – we think we are being individualistic, but in our designer clothes we become socially invisible.

Jesus called Peter to 'fish for people' (Mark 1:17, NLT). People who fish, often men, become aware, attentive. They watch and can read the signs of the water. They can do this for hours. Jesus asks Peter to switch this capacity to be attentive to the world of people; setting before them the dazzling, spinning, elusive and hidden reality of the kingdom.

This switching of our attention is much harder to do than we realise. This, too, is part of the mechanism of being mindful. When we are caught up in our thoughts we forget what we were trying to pay attention to, and are swept away in the thought-stream. Noticing that this has happened and switching our attention back to our intended focus is a key skill.

However, we all have this natural capacity of awareness and attentiveness. Carpenters learn it when they begin to work with wood. Where have you developed this capacity?

Mark's theology of discipleship goes wider than just the disciples. His gospel is full of unimportant so-called 'minor' characters who exhibit aspects of true discipleship. This includes women as well as men. In fact, the gospel ends with women demonstrating true discipleship while the male disciples are conspicuous by their absence. As an exercise, you could list all the minor characters that appear in this short gospel.

As a gospel it is a tree of life that you can dwell in (Psalm 104:12). Read it as a mysterious, veiled invitation to you – to a venue that is hidden, to a treasure that is worth leaving home for.

Day 9: Volunteers – the working relationship

Mindfulness is not just about meditation. We can learn to pay attention wherever we are. We can practise being mindful in every area of life.

If we want to stand in the place where we might meet God, then we need to come to terms with the idea of helping others, of serving. One of the ways we can become aware of how shaped we are into the patterns of our culture is by our use of the word 'volunteer'.

There is a lot of talk in our church about the shortage of volunteers – to do children's work or to visit the elderly and so on. Sometimes a volunteer steps down from doing a job and no one comes forward. Then sometimes people say, 'Well, you're the minister, you're the paid staff, so you should do it.' I began to wonder how this word 'volunteer' became such a powerful part of our identity in church life. A lot of thinking in church life about being a volunteer is automatic and unquestioned – mindless, if you like.

So I looked up the word 'volunteer' in the concordance in the back of my NIV Study Bible. And there, between 'voice' and 'vomit', was a big gap. I expected to see the word in black and white, with lots of references, but it simply wasn't there.

I then thought I'd better check the Bible to see if there were lots of holes where someone had cut out all the references to the word 'volunteer', but there weren't any holes in the Word, just holes in our thinking.

What I was left with was the idea that we hide our true biblical identity behind the fig leaf of volunteerism. What are we left with when we remove that fig leaf and stop using the excuse, 'I can't do that, I am just a volunteer'?

I think we have to go back to one of the key biblical principles – the priesthood of all believers. I checked my Bible to see if it actually said in the original Greek 'the volunteerhood of all believers', or even better 'the occasional volunteerhood of all believers', but it doesn't.

We are all priests, all full-time workers. So why do we set aside some people and pay them? Well, it's not to annoy volunteers by paying someone to do something they do for nothing. It is simply that the early church recognised that it is helpful to set aside some people to enable them to be rich in time and talents in extending the kingdom, and helping Jesus build His church. There should be no resentment about this – if we really understand our true identity.

In the Old Testament, you became a priest by being anointed. Jesus became our High Priest by being anointed at His baptism. In the words of Peter:

> You know what has happened throughout Judea, beginning in Galilee after the baptism that John preached – how God anointed Jesus of Nazareth with the Holy Spirit and power, and how he went around doing good and healing all who were under the power of the devil, because God was with him.
> *Acts 10:37–38*

What does it mean to be a priest? I can't think of a better description than this: to be anointed with the Holy Spirit and power, and to go around doing good and healing because God is with us.

Do we have the same anointing as disciples? Paul writes in 2 Corinthians 1:21–22:

> Now it is God who makes both us and you stand firm in Christ. He anointed us, set his seal of ownership on us, and put his Spirit in our hearts as a deposit, guaranteeing what is to come.

What is our anointing? It is simply to go around doing good and healing all because God is with us, and we have been anointed with the Holy Spirit and with power.

Some people in our church want us to have a season where we cancel every activity so that we can rediscover this primary identity. I have a lot of sympathy with their request.

So destructive and false is this divide between paid staff and volunteers that I have even fantasised about writing a letter to every minister and paid member of staff in Baptist churches asking that we all resign from our jobs and pass a rule that no one is ever allowed to be paid again in a Baptist church, so that we have to recognise as churches that we truly are a priesthood of all believers, not an organisation of hirelings and occasional volunteers.

Our biblical mission is to be the priesthood of all believers, becoming like Jesus and doing the things Jesus did. Our shadow mission is that we have become organisations of hirelings and occasional volunteers.

Jesus Christ as priest offered 'for all time one sacrifice for sins ... because by one sacrifice he has made perfect for ever those who are being made holy' (Hebrews 10:12–14).

If we truly grasp the extent of His sacrifice we can never claim just to be volunteers.

Day 10: A personal crisis experience – the spiritual relationship

I received my call into the ministry 21 years ago in a crisis experience lying on the floor of a cattle shed at New Wine's annual conference in Shepton Mallet.

I felt God saying, 'Take up the word of God which is the sword of the Spirit.' At the same time I saw a picture of a hand holding up a sword or cross of light. Such crisis experiences, popularly known as being 'slain in the Spirit' are often in the news.

Gamaliel's principle of saying that if it is of human origin it will fail (Acts 5:38) is helpful in analysing outpourings. But I think we can also start praying, 'Lord send revival, and start with me.' Without responding with shallow romanticising or thoughtless condemnation, I also think we need to develop our thinking about the supernatural dimension to our faith.

In particular, I think we need to develop a theology of crisis, alongside our theology of process in the area of God's transformation of us.

I believe the Bible affirms that alongside this lifelong process of transformation, there are times when we have a 'crisis' experience like being 'slain in the Spirit'. That crisis experience might lead to conversion as with Paul (Acts 9:4). It might lead to an overwhelming sense of one's sinfulness as with Isaiah (Isaiah 6:5). It might lead to priests not being able to minister and congregations prostrating themselves as with the dedication of Solomon's temple (2 Chronicles 7). So what might the Holy Spirit be doing through such experiences that can be affirmed?

Some psychologists talk about 'safe emergencies' or a 'healing crisis' where people need to find the necessary turbulence to break through into new growth. I believe being 'slain in the Spirit' can be such a necessary experience. Paradoxically it is also often a 'safe' experience.

There are a number of reasons why in our culture we might need to experience such turbulence.

In our consumerist lifestyle we are overworked and underspiritual, often spending very little time listening to God. The part of us that recognises our desperate need to slow down may cooperate with the Holy Spirit, and so we find ourselves on the floor giving the 'three-mile-an-hour God' our full attention.

One of the most important changes in psychology recently is the recognition that we have a plural self. Counselling and psychotherapy have recently developed theories recognising the area of multiplicity within a person. Within us are many different parts.

So we have the phenomenon that part of us responds enthusiastically on Sunday morning, crying out, 'Lord, Lord!' while half an hour after the service another part of us is surfing the internet looking at pornography. Meanwhile the consumer part of us is refusing to countenance tithing because that would interfere with our pursuit of the economic good life.

The crisis of commitment in the church can be explained because only a part of us is engaged with the Word, while the multiplicity of other parts in us is engaged with the world.

It may be that only the dramatic intervention of falling down physically under the power of the Spirit can bring the multiplicity of parts within us into dialogue with God the Father, through Christ by the Spirit.

In life-span development theory, one of the later crises we can face is between 'generativity and stagnation'.[35]

---

[35] Leonie Sugarman, *Life-Span Development* (Hove: Psychological Press Ltd, 2001) p.96.

My experience of church life is that some religious people cope with the massive change in our society by rigidifying. Only a crisis experience where the fire of God's Spirit melts us can break through our calcified defences. God opens our awareness to new possibilities. His mindful grace opens our eyes when sometimes we are unable to open them ourselves.

The question has been asked as to whether we live amongst one of the most 'me' generations ever. I think we do. One of the manifestations of this is people's desire to control their lives. Part of the commitment crisis in churches reflects this unwillingness to surrender to God's will.

Lying on the floor is an appropriate cultural expression of our surrender to God's control, in a culture where controlling our own lives is such a powerful value.

Since that first crisis experience with God, I know I have stood many times as rigid as a stone resisting God's grace. In the last few years, God has done a new work in me through process channels of grace like the Jesus Prayer and *Lectio Divina*.

Spending my formative years at boarding school helped me to be self-sufficient and emotionally unexpressive, like many in our culture. God's gracious work in process has removed some of those defences and enabled my heart and my mind to come together in a much more integrated way.

A few years ago I stood whilst an Anglican vicar came to pray for me. I didn't expect anything but he placed his hand on my heart and began to pray for me. It was like being hit by an electric shock and I bent forwards. He put his other hand on my back to steady me and I fell to the ground on my knees and began to weep.

One of the things I began to weep for was the previous hardness of my heart and for being content with my small experience of God when I could have asked to be filled 'to the measure of all the fulness of God' (Ephesians 3:19). It felt like being touched by God and touching God.

Here we see the spiritual at work, through the freely given grace of God. But I still had to stand in the place where I might possibly meet God. It is in that place and through that experience that my eyes were opened to consider a new reality. I was no longer to be a bank manager and have a career, and ever-bigger houses and cars. I was to have less and more, much more.

Day 11: Learning to be real through enchantment

Fairy tales, of which fantasy books are a central genre, are of crucial meaning and importance. So says the great, late psychoanalyst Bruno Bettelheim in his award-winning book *The Uses of Enchantment*.

Bettelheim's principal argument is that 'our greatest need and most difficult achievement is to find meaning in our lives'.[36] In his view, nothing is as enriching as the folk fairy tale because the central function of the enchantment of these stories is to help children and adults alike to discover meaning.[37] He says this not as someone who lived a life of seclusion in an academic, ivory tower but, having survived the concentration camps of Dachau and Buchenwald during the Second World War, as someone who was entirely aware of the brutal realities of the real world.

Intuitively, and from my own experience, I know Bettelheim's argument for the significance of meaning to be true. Our inner life can be a 'Perilous Realm', to quote J. R. R. Tolkien, and I've found myself, to rephrase him, behind the gates of this inner land with the key lost.[38] As a child, and even as an adult, the enchantment of fantasy genre books has given me a unique key to the gate of my own inner meaning.

However, I think the perilous realm of enchantment is all too often neglected when 'serious' literature is discussed. It is often dismissed as being a genre just for children, as if a book that can speak to a child could not also have a message for adults. This is one of the reasons why I have written a

---

[36] Bruno Bettelheim, *The Uses of Enchantment* (London: Penguin, 1991), p.3.
[37] Ibid, p.5.
[38] J. R. R. Tolkien, *Tree and Leaf* (London: Harper Collins, 2001), p.3.

children's fantasy book – *Flat Earth Unroofed* – *a tale of mind lore* – which is explicitly not just for the young.

Although I have been reading fairy stories and fantasy books since the age of three, I didn't write this book for the literature market but rather for my inner child. Before the rise of psychology and therapies, human beings told strange stories to bring healing and meaning. Fairy tales are amongst the most ancient tales told; they endure because of their timeless ability to touch our inner lives.

First and foremost, *Flat Earth Unroofed* is a story. But it is a tale that treats the ancient mind lore of awareness, attention and mindfulness as a worthy subject of narrative because it is part of the fabric of being. This is not a didactic tool but an exploration of often lost hidden realities.

Secondly, the hero and heroine are soul warriors who can bleed. They are wounded inwardly and suffer from anxious and depressed thoughts, and they battle to find the resilience to overcome them, just like many young people today. This is portrayed as normal and real: psychological distress should not be stigmatised in literature any more than it should be stigmatised in life.

Some people understand fairy stories and fantasy books; other people don't. One person who definitely understood the genre was J. R. R. Tolkien, who believed that the appeal of fairy tales, for both writer and reader, was that they take you into a world of 'sub-creation'.[39] My belief is that this world of sub-creation stimulates sub-creation within us, enabling us to imagine possibilities of meaning for our own lives. *Flat Earth Unroofed* imagines a post-religious, post-apocalyptic world of enchantment that enables us to face the dragons that lurk within our own hearts.

---

[39] Ibid., p. 47.

Many children and young people now live in an online world. This virtual conceit is not a modern fairy tale that connects them with their inner selves but rather is a captivating lie that distances them from reality. We need to re-enchant them with the real world which, paradoxically, can be found most vividly and clearly in the pages of a fairy tale or a fantasy book.

I have included a chapter of *Flat Earth Unroofed* at the end of this book for you to read if you would like to.

Day 12: Correcting the distortion of ageism

Read Mark 11 (read it mindfully, and ask yourself what are your automatic thoughts about ageing)

In Mark's gospel, Jesus gathers to Himself a disparate community. He attracts and seeks out people who are nobodies, easily dismissed by the world. He calls fishermen, a tax-collector called Levi (Mark 2:14); women who were not allowed to be witnesses in court followed Him. The blind, the deaf, the lame and the demon-possessed were all invited into the kingdom. Jesus corrected the distortions in His culture – those who were denied community and justice. Some of the same distortions exist in our culture. For example, there is the distortion of ageism. We need to become aware of these distortions and challenge them.

Everyone wants to live a long time but no one wants to get old. At least, that is the impression TV's obsession with youth gives us.

Winter would appear to be the cruellest season of life, but is it? There is something beautiful about a tree bare in winter, not needing all the unnecessary things we hang on our branches in the earlier seasons of life.

Is there another story than the media-inspired one of grumpy old men and women?

The psalmist tells us that those who walk with God will bear fruit even in old age (92:14), and Psalm 1 suggests that whatever season of life we are in, we will bear fruit if we are walking, standing or sitting with God.

What's the best way to look for the fruit in each season? One of the best ways is to review our east, west, north and south windows in each season.

The east window is where the sun rises, and we look for new beginnings – that which is rising above the horizon.

The west window, where the sun sets, is about things dying off, things to let go of and grieve for. In the winter of life it is easy to see only this window, because there may seem to be many losses and aspects of our life that are sinking below the horizon, a horizon that may seem all too near.

The north window is our compass, the foundations and values of our life that give us direction and consistency. One of the privileges of being part of a community of all ages over a long period of time is the relationships made with the different generations. I often find that my older, wiser friends have a strong north window, a clear sense of their values, which they live out.

Many people from younger generations seem to have a north window that fades in and out of their life. Our current culture encourages a lack of commitment in community and disposability in relationships.

The south window is the place of warmth that brings creativity and intimacy. In our double-glazed, centrally heated houses we forget the wisdom of 'south-facing' gardens. In the northern hemisphere, south-facing areas receive the sunshine. Nature knows this. If you want to find White Admiral butterfly eggs, look on south-facing ridges under south-facing leaves!

Whatever season of life we are in, if we review our lives through these windows we can regain a hopeful perspective on life. Churches can look at their current season of life through these windows. People who are married and in relationships can look at their journey together in a fresh way.

Marriages that lack the south-facing window of warm affection and intimacy are often stuck in deep and denied conflict whatever the surface calm. Such marriages are vulnerable to another person offering one of the partners a warm south window to bask in.

Each season of life, as well as having its fruit, has its own Seasonal Affective Disorder (SAD). The midlife crisis of late summer and early autumn is one of the most well known. It can often be found in the window that is out of balance with all the others. In the winter season of life, it might be about focusing solely on the west window and forgetting the existence of the other windows.

The testimony of many older Christians is that as the horizon of death comes closer in the west window, so Christ comes nearer with His light in the east window.

There is fruit to bear in any season of life. One of the most challenging passages in Mark is the cursing of the fig tree (Mark 11:12–14, 20–21). This is what scholars call an 'enacted' parable. Jesus didn't just speak out parables; He enacted them and revealed things through what He did, although these things are often mysterious, ambiguous and veiled.

In what is called a Markan sandwich, in between these two parts of the fig tree story, is the story of the clearing of the Temple.

Read Mark 11 now. Write down what you think the story might be saying to you. One of the problems in pulling parables to bits and explaining their exact meaning is that we miss the point of the parable. We will look next week at Mark's use of Jesus' parables in His theology of discipleship, awareness and revelation.

One clue for us is that we have a front-stage where we behave as the world thinks we should behave, but Jesus is interested in what is happening back-stage.

Day 13: Repairing the wounds through silence

Reread Mark 1:35–39

When we carry feelings of anxiety, worry and stress, as life and people hunt us down, we need to withdraw into silence and solitude in order to pray. It may be that Sundays do not offer this to us. The very thing that can repair us is often hard to find.

Much of today's worship and prayer seems to be a closed system which does not allow for the validity of silence and solitude. I have been in that place myself where people told me silence and solitude was important. I tried it, but it did not seem to work. But the work of silence and solitude may be the most important thing we do as disciples of the Still One.

If you look at things in the world slightly differently, you can see how silence and stillness is built into the fabric of existence around us.

At the beginning of everything, God spoke into the silence. From the beginning of our lives we have the connected silence and solitude of the womb, where the first sounds a baby will hear are the mother's heartbeat and the sound of her blood pumping at around 16 weeks, two months before the ears are fully formed.

The mysterious process of quiet sleep is a place of silence and solitude, and it makes up a third of our life. And yet so many people are stuck in doing and cannot access the place of being that is sleep. The silence and stillness of a spider, or a crouching tiger, are God-given signs in the world that we just don't see. Silence is more important to our well-being than we realise.

The attentiveness we develop in art or poetry which makes the world more fully present is another sign God has placed in the world to draw our attention to the importance of stillness.

That state of mindfulness can be accessed without meditation, and the work of Harvard psychologist Ellen Langer has focused on this important aspect. Meditative practices are very important because they change the activity and structure of our brains, but they are not the only route to a mindful place within.

Not being able to find a place of silence, for example for tinnitus sufferers, can feel like a madness. We live in a kingdom of noise where there is almost nowhere to go to find silence. We are drowning in noise but we do not know it: we think we are waving.

A small amount of silence can be wonderful, but stretch it out a bit and suddenly it becomes a fearful place. A number of times in prayer meetings I have said, 'Let's wait on God in silence', and within 20 seconds someone prays out loud.

The Desert Fathers, whose work was silence, tell us that a prolonged period of silence and solitude means we will have to 'wrestle with our inner demons'. In fact, when Abbot Moses was asked for a word of life he replied, 'Go and sit in your cell, and your cell will teach you everything.'[40] In other words, the silence and solitude of the cell will teach you everything.

Silence and solitude do not help us avoid experience; they help us face the inner experiences we have avoided: thoughts, emotions, sensations, distorted narratives – even our own self.

Silence and solitude, especially within monastic settings, has often been criticised as a withdrawal from life. But it is in silence and solitude that we also become aware of our connectedness to all things, as well as our inner demons. It is

---

[40] Benedicta Ward (tr.) *The Desert Fathers: Sayings of the Early Christian Monks* (London: Penguin, 2003) p.10.

in the kingdom of noise that we feel isolated and disconnected.

When Jesus healed the paralytic in Luke 5 He was able to read the hearts of the Pharisees and teachers of the law. This is often attributed rightly to a prophetic gifting through the Holy Spirit, but just before this passage we read, 'Jesus often withdrew to lonely places and prayed' (verse 16). It was that work of silence and solitude that enabled Him to read hearts.

I have only begun to put the tiny crescent of a fingernail into the doorway of silence and solitude, which is how we develop a contemplative self. It is a tiny splinter of sunlight in my heart that refuses to leave.

The goal of developing our contemplative self is to become awake and aware and compassionate like Jesus. The fourth century Syrian Ephrem said that in baptism we 'put on the Wakeful One'. Noise puts us to sleep; silence and solitude awaken us to be like the 'Wakeful One' we have put on.

Perhaps the most important thing is that silence and solitude are our umbilical cord to God. Just like babies, we can hear without having to hear through our ears. Without that guiding thread we lose our way in the competitive maze that is Western culture.

We are so preoccupied in our minds with our own selfish chatter we have forgotten how to listen to God with our hearts; we do not know how to hear the words He tries to form in our inner being.

Another way of saying that we wrestle with our inner demons in silence and solitude is to say that the illusions about who we are are stripped away.

If the voices saying that silence and solitude are the turning point in Christian transformation are right, then we need to find a way to encourage all Christians to embrace the vision.

In that silence and solitude we are 'blessed' with the greatest blessing of all – the gaze of a loving God and His loving presence when we 'take to heart' the word of God that has been revealed to us (Revelation 1:3).

The greatest challenge facing the church today is to encourage all Christians to take to heart this landscape of interior solitude, planting within it the transforming Word of God.

Go back to Mark 1:35–38 and read the words about Jesus going to a quiet, solitary place. It needs to become part of the rhythm of daily life. Orchestras tune up before a concert, not afterwards, and so, whoever we are, we need first thing each day to find a time and space of quiet and solitude and allow God to quietly repair us, as well as to access our own capacity for self-healing.

Day 14: Correcting a distorted view of Jesus and men

Read Mark 3:20–35

According to some recent research, there will be no men in the church in this country by 2028 at the current rate of loss. One of the problems is that they are presented with a distorted, feminised portrait of Jesus. One of the keys to bringing men back to the kingdom and the church is to rediscover a lost portrait of Jesus: He is not gentle Jesus, meek and mild; He does not float around in a nightgown.

Mark's gospel offers us a neglected title for Jesus, one that speaks powerfully to men. Jesus is called the 'one more powerful' by John the Baptist (Mark 1:7). In the Greek He is literally 'the stronger one'.

Who does this make Jesus like? This echoes the portrayal of Yahweh as divine warrior in Isaiah's new exodus theology. Mark's gospel employs the same root Greek word that is used in the Septuagint version of Isaiah 40:10. Yahweh comes with power in that verse, with the sense of being the more powerful one, the stronger one. In Isaiah 49 Yahweh will contend with fierce warriors and take plunder and captives from them.

It is this language that Jesus picks up when He is accused by the teachers of the law of being possessed by Satan: 'By the prince of demons he is driving out demons' (Mark 3:22). Jesus calls them to Him and speaks to them in an important parable.

No one, He says, can 'enter a strong man's house and carry off his possessions unless he first ties up the strong man. Then he can rob [plunder] his house' (Mark 3:27). Satan is the strong man here; it is the same root Greek word which describes Jesus as 'the stronger one'. As the stronger one, Jesus is the divine warrior who has come to bind the strong man and plunder his house and his kingdom.

Jesus bound Satan in His encounter with him in the desert (Mark 1:13), and the first miracle recorded by Mark is the driving out of an evil spirit (Mark 1:21–27). Jesus has already demonstrated the truth of His parable, that He has bound Satan and is now plundering his kingdom.

But it is on the cross that He completes His eschatological victory over Satan, death and sin. Christ the divine warrior as Victor needs to be rediscovered. That victory, won in principle, needs now to be won in reality in the present through hard conflict. Men who are caught in bitter existential battles with lust, greed, power and the slavery of the economic system – who are caught in addictions to pornography, alcohol, drugs and the emptiness of competing in the arena of consumerism – need to hear the language of the strong man being bound in their lives. This language needs to be part of their spiritual rebirth. This is a journey out of mindless living, where we are stuck in automatic thinking, or in avoidance of our real issues; it is a journey into self-awareness and mindfulness.

Alcoholics Anonymous, which began as a Christian movement, understands the importance of calling on the power of a 'stronger one' to be set free from addiction, acknowledging one's own powerlessness to change.

In our own denominational baptismal vows we retain the important language of renouncing the powers of evil. In the Orthodox tradition this ancient understanding is retained even more powerfully. Perhaps we need to strengthen even further the words of our baptismal liturgy.

In my pastoral experience, helping men use the language of binding the strong man in their spiritual life is very important – asking them what is the strong man that needs binding? Which inner demon afflicts them the most, to use the language of the earliest Christian psychologists, the Desert Fathers?

The afflictive thoughts they identify are still the ones that need wrestling with: gluttony, lust and greed; anger, sadness and acedia; vanity and pride. We may have opened the door to Christ, but very often we fail to close the door to Satan; very often we fail to close the door on our sinful thought patterns.

Our rationalistic culture dismisses the reality of spiritual warfare. Some charismatics focus too much on individual demonic activity. We seem to have lost sight of the deep theology of what Jesus is teaching here. What does Satan seek to do? In the language of Jesus in Mark's gospel, Satan makes us spiritually blind and spiritually deaf; he makes us hard-hearted. Jesus says to the disciples after the dazzle of kingdom miracles, 'Do you still not see or understand? Are your hearts hardened?' (Mark 8:17).

We need to be ransomed from this slavery, rescued from the kingdom of darkness into the kingdom of light.

As warriors in the likeness of Christ, we are to be fishers of men, women and children – an image Jeremiah used in the context of war (Jeremiah 16:16). A common Jewish idea of the time was about the 'nets of Satan'. Jesus' use of this image is not a sentimental one. It is about the rescue of people from the nets of Satan into the nets of the kingdom. It is an urgent image.

We need to go back to Scripture to recapture the true image of Jesus and men, and we need to go back to more ancient traditions than our own to challenge our thinking.

Week Three

Day 15: The parabolic

Memorise a parable in Mark, perhaps the parable of the sower in Mark 4:1–9. Read it mindfully. Stay with it all week.

Reading a parable should be like riding a unicycle across a tightrope between two different but connected levels of reality: it should be nerve-wracking, uncertain, apparently crazy, and yet, when you look back and see that you have arrived home, exhilarating. Too often we vandalise parables by pulling them apart, as if we can understand a flower by pulling all the petals off.

The parables are central to understanding the patterns of life Mark is weaving in his gospel. Jesus doesn't just use words in a parabolic way; some of His parables are what have been called 'enacted' parables. His very actions are parabolic.

What is a parable? A parable is designed to catch our attention because it is strange. It is designed to make us pay attention to the world and our understanding of it – and often points to the spiritual level of reality that is connected but distinct from the material level of reality around us. It should help us to think new things and heighten our level of awareness and discernment. A parable is often capable of many meanings. The mysterious cursing of the fig tree in Mark 11 is an enacted parable. Jesus' triumphal entry into Jerusalem on a colt in Mark 11 is an enacted parable.

In order to understand parables, we need to develop the open awareness and discerning awareness of watchfulness that Jesus commands and models.

Why does Jesus teach in parables, and why does Mark make them so central to his gospel? One idea is that the parables are modelling reality. Reality itself, and the way the two levels of reality of the spiritual kingdom and our ordinary everyday life interact, is mysterious. As Jesus says to His disciples in explanation (or not) of the parable of the sower, 'The secret of the kingdom of God has been given to you' (Mark 4:11).

The parable leads you on a thread, suspended over a chasm of possible misunderstandings into a new reality, awareness and thinking. Psychologists are now using paradoxical metaphors and stories to help people do the same thing in the modern world, much as Jesus did with parables. Jesus was unique in His development of this traditional form of riddles and stories within Judaism and the first-century world.

Jesus Himself makes the point that parables are as much about concealing revelation as revealing it. He says that He teaches in parables so that outsiders 'may be ever seeing but never perceiving' (Mark 4:12). Revelation itself is mysterious, veiled and ambiguous – and the parables mirror and model that reality.

Treasure is not found lying around on the surface; it is only found by alert watching. If revelation is mysterious, then, His command to be attentive and alert becomes central to the task of discipleship. Through paying attention to the parables we can be moved into a new place of awareness.

It is because of this that some scholars argue that Jesus Himself is a living parable of the kingdom, and that even the gospel of Mark as a whole is parabolic. Jesus came to make us aware of the reality of the kingdom of God, of the way the visible world around us points to the invisible presence of God who is seeking us.

If like the disciples, understanding does not come naturally or quickly, then, one of the implicit values in Mark is that of humility. Another value is not to be quick to judge others – we need to say 'I could be wrong' much more frequently than we do.

Day 16: A working relationship with learning

(in conversation with Professor Guy Claxton)

Write out Ephesians 3:14–19 on a piece of card and keep it with you.

The disciples in Mark's gospel have to unlearn many things – for example, what it means to be a disciple, or a Messiah. They have to learn new things – how to pray for healing, cast out demons, witness when in front of hostile authorities.

I have always loved learning but I know many people who have no confidence in themselves as learners. And yet it is one of the primary aspects of being a disciple – a disciple is always a learner. However, it is not just about us. We have to be concerned about our children and the children of others. Because the future will belong to learners, and to no one else.

Guy Claxton is Professor of the Learning Sciences at the University of Winchester. One of his most recent books is *What's the point of school? Rediscovering the heart of education.*[41] I first came across his writings while studying counselling at Roehampton University. Although he has many invitations to speak from around the world he agreed to come and speak at Stanmore Baptist on the theme of creativity.

I next came across him through his connection to my son's secondary school, Wren Academy in North Finchley, which specialises in Design and the Built Environment and is sponsored by the Church of England and Berkhamsted School. One of the things that excited us about the school is their adoption of Professor Claxton's learning philosophy.

---

[41] Guy Claxton, *What's the Point of School* (Oxford: Oneworld Publications, 2008).

I spent an afternoon at the school's new state-of-the-art facilities talking to him. Through his work he has issued a compelling wake-up call to the current educational system in this country.

His critique cannot be dismissed as 'fluffy liberal nonsense'; it is well founded in research and is enormously relevant not just to education and to the economy but also, intriguingly, to spirituality.

Professor Claxton is at the forefront of those arguing that the tail of assessment is wagging the dog of education and learning. Other elements of his diagnosis of the ills of our educational system are equally relevant to Christians in their role as educators, citizens and spiritual beings.

One of the problems he identifies in education policy that crosses over into the world of the church is the simplification of what are actually complex issues. For example, in the Christian world, the viewpoint that says 'Islam is of the devil so let's burn Korans' is a very dangerous simplification. A seriously damaging simplification in the world of education is the dominant concept of the fixed nature of ability: 'It's not even as obvious as whether I believe I've got a big bucket of intelligence or a medium-sized bucket, or a small bucket. It's whether I see intelligence as a bucket-like kind of thing. Buckets come in different sizes but the real problem is the belief that once I've got one I won't get a bigger one.'

What Professor Claxton argues is that young people's learning capacity can be stretched. Children can learn to be gifted. The downside of being told one only has a 30-watt mind is obvious, but what is less understood is the negative impact of trying to live up to the expectations of being told one has a 100-watt mind. Such talented and gifted students are often not resilient about failure, and can suffer from Imposter Syndrome, fearing their cleverness will be exposed as a fraud.

His case against the current education system is powerfully supported by a 2009 report commissioned across 25 countries by EdExcel, the education group, entitled *Effective Education for Employment*.[42] 'This report was a road to Damascus experience. Everybody said the same thing: education is not fit for purpose. It doesn't equip people for life or for employment,' says the Professor.

This disconnect between our education systems and the needs of twenty-first-century life should concern the church. How much have our own education systems mirrored uncritically the patterns of our society?

But just as his work is 'brightening' up the future of learning, we have a theology of learning that also has that capacity. For example, in 1 Corinthians 8 Paul distinguishes between knowledge, seen as a static, completed state, which 'puffs up' and knowing as a continuous process of ever-learning.

Jesus said, 'Blessed are the meek, for they will inherit the earth' (Matthew 5:5). The humble are learners and they shall inherit the future.

Are you a resilient learner, or do you believe that you are fixed in your ability? Write down Ephesians 3:14–19, which ends 'that you may be filled to the measure of all the fulness of God', and reflect today on those words. We have an infinite capacity to learn if we can be filled with all the fullness of God. We need to be resilient, because often we are slow to learn and need perseverance and repetition in order to succeed.

---

[42] Jim Playfoot & Ross Hall, *Effective Education for Employment* (Edexcel, 2009).

Day 17: Practising the presence of God – developing the spiritual relationship

Just before my first sabbatical some years ago, I was very anxious and close to burnout. I knew I needed to find my way out of this difficult place. The prayer that led me back to the presence of God was the Orthodox prayer known as the Jesus Prayer. Simon Barrington-Ward, the former Bishop of Coventry, helped me greatly with his books on the Jesus Prayer, and spent some time talking to me about his friendship with Brother Ramon, another exponent of the Prayer.

Former Baptist minister Raymond Lloyd, who became better known as Franciscan monk and writer Brother Ramon, had a gift for friendships which embraced people from lorry drivers to Anglican bishops. He and Simon Barrington-Ward co-wrote a book called *Praying the Jesus Prayer Together*,[43] which came out shortly after Ramon's death from cancer in June 2000. The Jesus Prayer – 'Lord Jesus Christ, Son of God, have mercy on me, a sinner' – has scriptural roots, was developed by the Desert Fathers and was taken up and preserved by the Orthodox church before it began to move west.

Bishop Simon visited Brother Ramon a number of times at Glasshampton Monastery where Ramon lived out his vocation as a hermit. They had both been praying and teaching on the Jesus Prayer as a way of 'practising the presence of God', to use Brother Lawrence's memorable phrase.

Brother Ramon felt it right that they should meet for a week to practise, teach and share the Jesus Prayer, not only for

---

[43] Simon Barrington-Ward & Brother Ramon, *Praying The Jesus Prayer Together* (Oxford: BRF, 2001).

themselves, but ultimately perhaps for a wider audience. It was out of this week their joint book on the Jesus Prayer was born.

'Initially I rather kept the Jesus Prayer to myself; I felt I was very much a beginner,' says Bishop Simon. 'My spiritual director told me I should teach it in the diocese; he felt it was something really needed.

'Out of this came a little book called *The Jesus Prayer* which Brother Ramon read, and that's when he invited me to his hermitage. I was quite nervous about meeting a hermit, but he was so genial. It was just like meeting someone in a pub.'

It was at their third meeting that Brother Ramon broached the subject of writing a book together on the Jesus Prayer. Ramon believed the Holy Spirit would show them in a week of praying together what the book was to be about.

A few months earlier Brother Ramon had been discovered to have prostate cancer and during this week of prayer was in a great deal of pelvic pain.

'That dimension of pain, somehow, in an extraordinary way, deepened the time very much and there was something very profound about it, and the feeling that really he might be journeying beyond this life.

'Brother Ramon had a replica of St Francis' San Damiano crucifix which shows Christ in glory and yet in pain – a fusion of the two – and the week had that same fusion. It was about becoming closer to Christ and receiving His amazing love and being sent out. It's a receiving which is always a sending.'

Part of the fruit of using the Jesus Prayer as a vehicle for practising the presence of God for Bishop Simon is this awareness of being loved, receiving that and then being sent out.

'I see this as a clear sign of the Holy Spirit taking and using this prayer to move us deeper and wider,' says Bishop Simon.

Soon after that week, Ramon was moved back into the main house at Glasshampton so that he could be looked after. He had feared when he felt so ill that he wouldn't be able to write any more. But with the pain controlled he improved in health and was able to write all of his share of the chapters of the new book.

Bishop Simon suddenly received a message late in May 2000 from Glasshampton that Brother Ramon had taken a turn for the worse, and went to make one last visit. 'He said to me that Christ had come to him across a bridge and began to take him and Ramon said, "No, I've got my sister coming on Saturday and Simon's coming tomorrow, can He wait?"' adds Bishop Simon, laughing.

Sitting by Brother Ramon impressed Bishop Simon more than any other deathbed he has attended, and gave him a new confidence about dying himself. It was then that Brother Ramon handed Bishop Simon the parcel of his finished writing for the planned new book on the Jesus Prayer.

'I said how strange it was to be saying goodbye in this life and that I wouldn't see him any more after this. He grasped my hand with a twinkle in his eye and said, "This is the last journey, you know. But when we get to the end of this – there'll be..." and he said this with almost a shout, "a Big HULLO!" We parted really merrily after all.'

Mark's gospel doesn't offer easy answers or cheap grace. The way of discipleship is the way of the cross. Jesus says, 'If anyone would come after me, he must deny himself and take up his cross and follow me' (Mark 8:34). This is the way of God; the path to glory goes through the place of pain and suffering. Contemplative practices like the Jesus Prayer help us stay with the pain and the suffering and transcend them.

Day 18: Real discernment

Mark's Jesus is a deeply human one. In one of His first healings a man with leprosy comes to Him and begs Jesus on his knees to heal him. Mark tells us that Jesus was 'filled with compassion' (1:41). Throughout Mark's gospel Jesus is modelling the migratory route home to God that we are to follow. We need real discernment to find out what patterns of the world we are shaped in. One of those patterns is that of competition.

The true enemy of compassion is not indifference but competitiveness. This thought has haunted me following a dream I had recently. The pages of a Bible were blowing in the wind until my eye caught sight of a silver-plated passage, the words raised up like Braille. I knew I had to read the words that were leaping off the page.

The word that glittered was 'compassion'. Paul declares that God is the 'Father of compassion' (2 Corinthians 1:3). The Old Testament tells us that being compassionate is part of God's name (Exodus 34:6–7). The Hebrew word for compassion, *rachamim*, has at its root the word 'womb'. That's why God can say to Isaiah with compassion, 'As a mother comforts her child, so will I comfort you' (Isaiah 66:13).

This deep and powerful emotion is at the root of Jesus' healing ministry. The Greek expression *splangchnizomai* conveys this gut-level feeling, and is used many times of Jesus, the man for others 'moved with compassion'.

Compassion is at the heart of what moves God to be 'God with us', and to be God who suffers with us, and to be God who feels our hunger, sickness, pain and loss as if it were His own.

It is clear from the signs of the times that competitiveness dominates men and women as a distorted pattern of this world. In part, it may be as a result of the Thatcher revolution of the 1980s. It seems in schools and hospitals, as well as workplaces up and down the country, that much creativity, compassion and holistic thinking has been sacrificed on the altar of competitive efficiency.

The government's intransigence over the plea for all Gurkha soldiers to have an equal right of residence in this country was a sign of its competitive way of being combating the compassionate way of being expressed by Joanna Lumley and others. BBC1's *The Apprentice* is a horrifyingly naked expression of competitiveness.

This is a huge problem for us as Christians, with our culture shaping us to be competitive and the Bible calling us to be compassionate. It is clear, even in the church, which way of being is winning. Henri Nouwen compared us to pencils with a small rubber on the end; the pencil is our competitiveness, and the small rubber is the amount of compassion we feel and exercise, rubbing out our mistakes.

Like the church in Corinth, too many congregations are marked by competitive factions, critical and judgmental attitudes which require the suppression of our compassion, and feelings of being superior to those outside the church walls.

A recent article in *Christianity Today* suggested that Scrooge is alive and well and living within Christianity in the USA, with 36 per cent of Evangelicals giving away less than two per cent of their income. My guess is that in this country, too, when the plate is passed round, many pass to others the buck of giving.

The temptation for organisations and churches in the current climate of fear and economic crisis will be to become more competitive and less compassionate.

Jesus said, 'You must be compassionate, just as your Father is compassionate' (Luke 6:36, NLT). My fear is that our veneer of compassion will wash off very quickly as economic hardship digs deeper.

Now is the time, counter-intuitively, to seek the same anointing of the Holy Spirit that launched Jesus' ministry, and enabled Him to 'compassionately' comfort all who mourn.

We need to ask God to touch our lips with the burning coals of His truth, so that we cry out, 'Woe is me, I am competitively uncompassionate, and belong to a competitively uncompassionate people.'

The Greek text says literally that, when Jesus was baptised, the Holy Spirit entered 'into' Him (Mark 1:10). We also need that interior work. In Luke 17:21 Jesus says, 'The kingdom of God is within you.' That is where the deep transforming work of being remade needs to happen. This kingdom of God is compassionate. As Christians we haven't made enough of this gospel truth. The power of compassion is being rediscovered in mindfulness therapies.

Day 19: The distortion of ecoalienation

Place is very important in Mark's gospel – the desert, the mountain, the sea. The mountain is the place of epiphany and encounter with God. Every time I spend time in the mountains I can feel myself coming alive physically, spiritually and emotionally, in a way that doesn't happen in everyday suburban life.

I've been privileged to visit the mountains regularly as chaplain for a group organised by fellow Baptist Clive Beattie who runs Gold Hill Holidays – a Christian outdoor activities ministry.

I have a sense that this periodic awakening is deeply significant. One aspect that contributes to it is the ethos of the holidays, which is not 'hotel Christianity', but more 'muscular Christianity'. The group travels out by coach, with the food and equipment required for a week in the mountains. An 18-hour coach journey requires patience and fortitude, but also helps bond the group in a way that flying wouldn't. Everyone has to help on one day of the week in preparation and serving of the meals.

The phrase 'muscular Christianity' was coined in 1857 in a review of a book by Thomas Hughes (1822–1896), author of *Tom Brown's Schooldays*, who was a strong advocate of the link between sport, exercise and the development of Christian character. Charles Kingsley (1819–1875) was another Victorian advocate of muscular Christianity, with an emphasis on pursuits such as fishing, hunting and camping. Implicit in this is the benefit of spending time in God's creation.

The strand I would like to tease out is the benefit of spending time in God's creation. My own experience of coming alive in mountains suggests there is something very important missing in suburban life.

One of the possibilities is what the late Howard Clinebell, pioneer of pastoral counselling, would call 'ecoalienation'. In a book called *Ecotherapy* he argues that ecoalienation happens to all human beings when we lose our connectedness with nature.[44] This is an idea which has theological merit and deserves further exploration from a Christian perspective.

This ecoalienation often goes unrecognised without the corresponding experience of ecobonding, like mine on the mountains.

The other common experience reported by people is, 'I feel closer to God in the mountains.' Mountains touch on our deeper alienation from God.

My concern with all of this is that ecoalienation is built into our Western consumerist culture.

One of the very helpful things I have seen in this one small ministry is the number of younger leaders that the founder Clive Beattie has encouraged and developed over the last 20 years.

It is not just our own physical, spiritual and emotional health that is at stake, though. Howard Clinebell argues that 'the most serious, most dangerous health challenge all of us in the human family face is to reverse the planet's continuing ecological deterioration.'[45]

In the mountains at times I have been made very aware of the fragility of the earth's ecosystem, with a shortage of snow, and unseasonal temperatures threatening the famous downhill skiing race in Wengen, known as the Lauberhorn.

Stanley Grenz points out in his book *Theology For the Community of God* that part of God's plan for us as the community of God's people is to live in harmony with all of

---

[44] Howard Clinebell, *Ecotherapy: healing ourselves, healing the earth* (London: The Haworth Press, 1996) p.26.
[45] Ibid., p.1.

creation.[46] Another important insight he outlines is that sin never just affects us alone; sin is our failure to live in community with God, with each other, and with the natural environment. What we also rediscover in our engagement with the natural world is our own embodiment; we come to our senses.

Our ecoalienation sleepwalks us towards an uncertain future. It is only an awakening of our connectedness to the earth that will enable us to navigate that future. For as Howard Clinebell puts it, 'our children will ask the world of us'.[47] But can we give it to them? One of the distortions is that we often don't even see that we are suffering from ecoalienation, or the part we are playing in the ecological crisis.

---

[46] Stanley J. Grenz, *Theology for the Community of God* (Carlisle: Paternoster Press, 1994).

[47] Howard Clinebell, *Ecotherapy: healing ourselves, healing the earth,* p.xi.

Day 20: Repairing our vision

Take yourself off to an art gallery this week.

Jesus in Mark's gospel had the eyes of an artist and the words of a poet. In other words, He had acute observational skills for seeing human life and its deeper realities. One of the things He was criticised for was not being religious, and doing many apparently unreligious things, especially on the Sabbath. In the West we are also guilty of separating the sacred from the ordinary, when according to Mark the sacred is found in the ordinary. That means we can develop awareness and attentiveness through apparently non-religious things like art and poetry.

This is mindfulness without meditation, using our innate capacity for awareness and attention wherever we are. Going to an art gallery reminds us that there is no sacred/secular divide, that areas of life like poetry and art point back to God. This aesthetic knowing can open doorways into the spiritual.

Apparently, when questioned about his *Water Lilies* paintings, Monet did not want to explain his art and wanted people to see in the paintings whatever they wished.

His comment came back to me when I came across one of the *Water Lilies* series, *Nympheas*, tucked away in the Tate Modern in an exhibition called *Material Gestures*, with other paintings representing Abstract Expressionism.

I don't know if I wished to see the things that came to mind as I gazed at it. But it seemed that Monet, by gazing at the water lily pond in his garden at Giverny from the 1890s to his death in 1926, moved from ordinary psychological awareness to a deeper spiritual awareness which was reflected in these paintings. As the canvases became room-sized, one wonders if they provide an insight into God's own creative vision as He created the infinite spaces of the galaxies.

Such is the lack of horizon and the infinite variations of light and colour, water and air, that what came to mind for me was the metaphor 'a cloud of unknowing'. Looking at this painting was like looking at a cloud of unknowing, but knowing that Monet had somehow pierced it and was representing a deeper reality beyond it. I had a sudden perception of my much more limited awareness, but had a great desire to follow Monet into a deeper awareness.

The unknown author of the fourteenth-century classic *The Cloud of Unknowing* says of God, 'by love he can be caught and held, but by thinking never'.[48] Monet painted out of love and has found for us a deeper reality than we could hope to see. This attitude of still focus that enabled Monet to transcend previous ways of seeing and painting is also our pattern that will bring us into awareness of God.

Where Monet went for love of water lilies, can we not go for love of God?

One of our problems is that we can apparently capture reality so precisely through photographs that we assume that is the only reality. This limits our ability to pierce that cloud of unknowing that is God. God is not a photograph, and cannot be photographed. Something of His reality can be perceived in a Monet painting of a water lily, because it cannot be contained and boundaried by the limited perception of photography, which has become our automatic way of looking at the world, and God, as if we could pin Him down.

The other pattern of reality that came to mind as I looked at the painting, and relooked at it, came out of the hundreds of tiny touches of the brush that make up the canvas. I was

---

[48] Clifton Wolters (tr.) *The Cloud of Unknowing and other Works* (Harmondsworth: Penguin, 1983) p.68.

reminded that quantum physics tells us that reality is not as solid as we perceive it, that actually we are made of dancing particles, strange and blue and charming.

We are given a hint that reality is less substantial than we observe with our senses in the resurrection accounts when Jesus passes through His grave clothes, or through a locked door.

If we want to be bathed in the beauty of something that approximates the wonder of the first morning and a walk with God, then we can lose ourselves in a Monet painting and find ourselves bathed in that elusive inbreaking of God's presence.

Such a painting of the heart is close to the prayer of the heart, both of which lead us to a luminous awareness of the glory of God. Take yourself off to an art gallery this week, or read or write some poetry. Perhaps try drawing or painting something from the world around you.

Day 21: The migrating journey

Memorise Mark 9:35. Stay with it all week; keep coming back to it.

We need to look at Mark's gospel as a whole, and not just in smaller sections. One of the themes you can trace through it is that it is a series of journeys. To help us reorientate ourselves to the journey of discipleship, we need to start at the beginning. Jesus walks by Simon and Andrew in the place of their work and says to them, 'Come, follow me' (Mark 1:16). They do, and we are given no explanation for this. Mark often reveals things by showing us, not telling us what is happening.

One analogy is that of imprinting. Fledgling birds follow the first thing they see, believing it to be their mother. There are examples of fledglings imprinting on humans. Made in the image of God, we are designed to imprint ourselves on God the first time we sense His numinous presence. Perhaps this is what happened here. The first time I met my wife I knew she was the one I wanted to marry. We didn't get married straightaway, but we began a journey together. In Mark we are always called into community with others.

However, because we are fallen, and we live in a fallen world, that capacity to imprint ourselves and follow God on a journey, to know how to navigate spiritually, has been damaged. In the film *Fly Away Home*, goslings who have lost their parents imprint on a young girl, who teaches them how to fly, and then leads them home on their migratory route – which they needed to learn from other geese but couldn't. We are like those birds: we need to relearn the route home to God.

The disciples' three-year journey with Jesus is about them learning that route. Jesus shows them the important places of sensing and orientation along the way. He models the journey. The beginning place of sensing and orientation is prayer in a solitary place (Mark 1:35–39). We learn best through repetition, just like young birds. The young birds have to learn to avoid the traps, nets and dangers along the way. There are two ways forward for the disciples: the way of the world, or the way of God; the rocky ground or the good soil.

He shows them the place of apparent success as they are sent out and we are told, 'They drove out many demons and anointed many sick people with oil and healed them' (Mark 6:13). Not understanding the geography of success, they start to argue about who is the greatest (Mark 9:33–34). The way of the world, the way fraught with danger, is the fearful saving of self, the gaining of the whole world, wanting to be the greatest.

In a paradoxical riddle that needs to be memorised (like the route) and meditated on until it becomes the magnetic field that we orient ourselves to, Jesus says, 'If anyone wants to be first, he must be the very last, and the servant of all' (Mark 9:35). Instead of trying to stand over this text and atomise its meaning, we need to allow it to work away mysteriously behind our awareness, until it becomes our awareness.

Paradoxically, it is the place of failure that opens the eyes. Peter needs to boast that he will not disown Jesus (Mark 14:29) and then disown Him (Mark 14:66–72) before light breaks in, and he breaks down and weeps in full awareness of who he is and what he has done.

In the beginning the numinous presence of Jesus cracked the defences of Simon and the light came in. Success blinded him and failure gave him new eyes to see.

The birds fly the same route again and again. We are to as well. Mark has given us the places of sensing, orientation and navigation to find our way home. But, like the young birds, we need to learn and we need help from those around us who know the way.

Spiritual practices like the Jesus Prayer or *Lectio Divina* that are repeated lay down a succession of new positive experiences that begin to change our brains and transform our minds. Just as marginal gains in sport can make a big difference over a period of time, so marginal gains through spiritual practices can do the same thing.

Week Four

Day 22: Jesus – master and commander of attention

In ironic contrast to the disciples, in Mark's gospel Jesus is the master and commander of attention. After His baptism, which may have been what opened His eyes, we read, 'As Jesus was coming out of the water, he saw heaven being torn open and the Spirit descending on him like a dove' (Mark 1:10). What He sees is more significant than we often realise, but here is the first time we see His spiritual awareness.

Jesus commands our 'watchfulness' at the end of the gospel, but He commands the attention of others in a different way as well. The eyes of people are drawn towards Him. The first disciples see Jesus walking on water and also swimming on land – there is something different about Him and they follow Him (Mark 1:18). Mysteriously, after His baptism He is endowed with authority, and it is probably from the Spirit. As mentioned earlier, in the original language of the text the Holy Spirit enters 'into' Him (1:10).

Jesus inhabits both the spiritual and physical realms, and even the demons recognise His authority and presence in the spiritual realm. 'What do you want with us, Jesus of Nazareth?' they cry (Mark 1:24). When He heals the paralytic, some teachers of the law are thinking judgementally of Jesus, and we are told, 'Immediately Jesus knew in His spirit that this was what they were thinking in their hearts' (Mark 2:8). This insider view is traditionally ascribed to a gift of discerning through the Holy Spirit. It is also a product of His spending time in prayer – the crucible of becoming aware.

However, we shouldn't dismiss what Jesus does here through this inside view as somehow not humanly possible. Trained counsellors and psychotherapists can pick up the thoughts and feelings in a room that are not theirs, because these things leak and we have an innate capacity for awareness.

We recognise the sort of attention and awareness Jesus is master of by noticing the other forms of watching that Mark shows us in his gospel. The Pharisees begin to watch Jesus closely, 'looking for a reason to accuse Jesus' (Mark 3:2). This suspicious, judgemental watching is not the watching that Jesus is commending.

In the parable of the sower at the beginning of His ministry, Jesus shows He is fully aware of how His ministry will be received – that there are different types of soil, many not receptive to His kingdom message. In Mark 12 Jesus sits opposite the Temple treasury and watches the crowd putting money in. The word for watching, *etheorei*, is an attentive sort of watching (verse 41). Mark uses the same word to describe the way the women are watching the crucifixion in Mark 15:40.

In Jesus' discourse to the disciples in Mark 13, where they are commanded to be discerning, watchful and openly aware, it is not to be done in an anxious way (verse 11). The watching Jesus commands is not the anxious watching of our twenty-first-century culture. It is not the competitive watching of 'who was the greatest' (Mark 9:34). It is not the acquisitive watching of our own emptiness, seeking to fill that with 'the whole world' (Mark 8:36).

There is also the paradoxical watchfulness of hearing. One of Jesus' constant refrains in Mark is, 'He who has ears to hear, let him hear' (4:9, 23; 8:18). Here we have the open awareness that is paying attention at many levels, with narrow, more discerning patterns of awareness – seeing, hearing, the sensing of the inside view which comes from another part of us, as well as being the divine gift of the Holy Spirit.

The consistent pattern of the disciples not seeing, hearing or understanding which continues right up to the end of the gospel, and Jesus' modelling of Himself as a master of attention throughout the gospel, lays the groundwork for the major emphasis on awareness, attentiveness and watchfulness in Mark 13 and 14. In looking at these three strands we can see that watchfulness is at the centre of what it means to be a disciple. Prayer is one of the central disciplines for achieving that watchfulness (Mark 14:38).

In Mark's gospel Jesus is the Mindful One. He laments that His disciples are not perceptive: they do not see or hear, or understand. But it is clear that the central part of being a disciple is to be perceptive and to be mindful – mindful of God, of others, of creation, and also of our own self.

Day 23: Working on our learning

(a personal conversation with Professor Guy Claxton)

As part of the implicit developing of our humility and seeing the way of God, Jesus takes a little child, stands him among the disciples and says, 'Whoever welcomes one of these little children in my name welcomes me' (Mark 9:36–37). This may well be another enacted parable.

One of those I have learnt much from in conversation is Professor Guy Claxton, who, as we discussed earlier, is out of the line of educational prophets who ask why we count qualifications but not the cost of acquiring them. He wishes to restore the spark of dangerous inquisitiveness into the person of the child as well as the practice of education. He believes this dangerous inquisitiveness should exist not only in education but also in what he calls 'proximal spirituality'.

For the professor, education is not just about skills and technical proficiency but also about the cultivation of qualities like inquisitiveness. He is a friend and advocate not only for children and parents but also for teachers whose own spark of dangerous inquisitiveness has been snuffed out by a controlling system.

'The culture in schools in the UK over the last 15 years or so has been one in which teachers have been continually told what to think and how to talk,' he says. 'So it's not surprising and it's not teachers' fault if they have developed in some places a bit of a mindset that says, "Tell me the answer, give me the formula... show me how to do it" rather than, "Give me enough to get going and then encourage me to think about it myself."'

His critique of government setting all the rules for teachers, and then teachers setting all the rules for children, is actually a wider critique of our culture of disempowerment. Jesus critiqued the disempowering culture of His day when He said, 'Let the little children come to me.' He was also treating a child as a person in their own right, rather than an un-person, or a person-in-the-making. His suggestion elsewhere about becoming like a little child underlines this.

Professor Claxton is similarly motivated by a concern for the person within the system, which is reflected in the key qualities he believes as essential to learning: things like independence, inquisitiveness, collaborativeness, reflectiveness, imagination, clear thinking, sociability of various kinds and empathy. These are all personal qualities.

I believe it is no coincidence that his learning philosophy is called Building Learning Power (BLP). Professor Claxton's approach takes children's reality seriously and seeks to empower them.

This requires a complete change of culture within schools. He has experienced scepticism and resistance from the powers that be, and also what he calls the 'tinsel' approach, where a few creative ideas are scattered on top of the existing tree of learning. But he has also experienced what he calls deep, interesting and challenging conversations where people actually question the whole tree of education with him.

Children who are innately dangerously inquisitive and personal are being labelled dangerous by our popular press. In a world and educational system that seeks to make them safe, they never learn how to exercise power properly. 'Street children' is a now a term for children out of the control of adults; we much prefer 'indoor' children.

Children need to be given space to use their inquisitiveness. Professor Claxton cites as an example North Finchley's Wren Academy, a specialist school where the library has been designed as the central hub of the school.

'In many schools you'd be hard pressed to find the library. But here it's a social area, it's a concourse, it's got nice interesting little places a child can curl up and read a book ... that sends powerful messages to youngsters about the pleasures of reading.'

Professor Claxton's critique also opens the door on to the rats in the cellar of the church.

We have too often been controlling. Too often we have told people what to think and in places we have neither empowered nor protected children. Sadly, in the eyes of the world, we have seemed to be inquisitor rather than inquisitive.

Scientism might be a flight from uncertainty, but faith as a more humble form of knowing should embrace uncertainty. This is mindful learning. We should not be know-it-alls treating people as know-nothings.

Children are very aware and attentive and often learn dysfunctional behaviours from the adults around them. Children have something to say. Let's listen to them, and let's learn from them as Jesus wished.

Day 24: More on the Jesus Prayer and the spiritual relationship

(in conversation with Bishop Simon Barrington-Ward)

I have learnt a lot about the Jesus prayer in conversation with Simon Barrington-Ward. It was Mother Teresa who said being unwanted, unloved, uncared for and forgotten by everybody is the greatest poverty of all. Simon Barrington-Ward believes the Jesus Prayer has the power to tackle this terrible relational poverty.

'Above all this is a prayer of being loved. It is not for fanatics or people who are extraordinarily holy. It is for all of us, being a way of prayer which is easy to use, and supremely about being loved and lifted up.' The bishop leans forward and his eyes light up as he emphasises this point.

The simple repetition of the words, 'Lord Jesus Christ, Son of God, have mercy on me, a sinner,' caught the popular imagination in the West in the 1960s, through J. D. Salinger's book *Franny and Zooey*. The young hippy-like characters try the prayer in the book as a type of mantra, without much success.

However, Bishop Simon acknowledges that one of the main obstacles to the prayer today is the thought of repeating a simple phrase. 'The key thing is to get people over the oddity of repeating a sentence, and once they do realise, which I have tried to explain in the book, it's not vain repetition, it's just another way in which the Spirit prays in us, like tongues.'

He makes the point that in Luke 18 it is the Pharisee who is guilty of vain repetition, not the tax collector, who prays simply from the heart.

Bishop Simon has done further research into the history of the Jesus Prayer, and talks about it animatedly. The Bible

Reading Fellowship has brought out a revised edition of his book *The Jesus Prayer*,[49] in which he incorporates some of this new research.

Initially he thought the Jesus Prayer was just one among many prayers that emerged from the Desert Fathers and Mothers, but now he believes that gradually this prayer emerged, at least by the second century of the desert movement, as potentially a primary way of praying. 'The movement out into the desert was a movement of those who wanted to reach out to the kingdom, to find something deeper for the whole church, which had grown very large and worldly.'

Bishop Simon believes that a number of strands came together in the fourth and fifth centuries, first through fourth-century teachers of prayer such as Macarius the Great, disciple of St Anthony, then in differing ways, through Evagrius of Pontus on the one hand and the writings of the unknown Syrian monk, strangely called 'Pseudo-Macarius (whose homilies so much appealed later to John Wesley), and eventually, supremely, in the fourth century through Bishop Diadochus of Photike in Greece.

Diadochus managed to draw together the two strands of thought: one influenced by Greek Platonism, and the other closer to Hebrew and Syrian influences. He brought them both together in the Jesus Prayer, which was contemplative, incarnational and biblical. It was a prayer shaped by Paul's command that we should 'pray continually' (1 Thessalonians 5:17). It drew upon the short repeated prayer of the tax collector in Luke 18, 'God, have mercy on me, a sinner,' and that of blind Bartimaeus at the end of the same chapter (also in Mark 10:46–52), 'Jesus, Son of David, have mercy on me!' These were short, persistent appeals and petitions that came

---

[49] Simon Barrington-Ward, *The Jesus Prayer*.

out of a sense of desperation and helplessness, still the basis of the prayer today.

Bishop Simon believes these early teachers of prayer were also led by the Holy Spirit to develop the Jesus Prayer after deep reflection on Jesus' words in John 15:4, 'Remain in me, and I will remain in you', and Paul's words in Philippians 1:21, 'For to me, to live is Christ'.

'Paul was obviously dwelling in Christ, and these people were looking to do the same,' says Bishop Simon. 'Being centred in Christ by the power of the Holy Spirit.'

It is the example of the tax collector and blind Bartimaeus, as well as his many years teaching the prayer, that encourages Bishop Simon to emphasise that the prayer is very much for beginners as well as those seeking to go deeper into prayer. His book helps people in both these categories.

Another piece of evidence revealing its biblical basis in the New Testament, and its place as a Spirit-shaped prayer, is the fruit its disciplined practice brings to people.

'This little prayer focuses on the person and presence of Jesus. This will always be concrete and incarnational. It will always be a plea for the presence and love of our Lord and Saviour to grasp hold of us more and more. And because it is being repeated, because you are focusing on the presence and not preaching yourself little sermons, you are actually being still.'

Bishop Simon argues that the prayer didn't emerge by accident, and that the fusion of contemplative and incarnational strands made it the main prayer for the monks by the fourteenth century, and central to the Orthodox church. 'And I think that was right, because it seemed to be something, if I can put it like this, both evangelical and also contemplative and mystical.'

Bishop Simon feels strongly that it is the presence of the risen Lord of John 20:19–21 we need to seek, when Jesus came to the disciples, as they huddled together in fear and at the end of themselves, with His transforming power – of which we too are always in need. This insight can help us in dealing with our sinful nature. He says, 'Don't worry about struggling with all your sins in particular. Practise the presence more and more deeply and it will cleanse your heart and gradually transform you. And I believe I've found it doing that myself.'

This is part of the biblical fruitfulness that Bishop Simon believes the prayer helps bring about. 'Any progress that I've made at all, and sometimes I don't feel I've made any, when I do sense or feel that I've overcome something that was besetting me a lot, I realise it was His presence doing it, not my trying of myself to tackle the same head on.'

For Bishop Simon, the prayer holds together two things at the heart of Christian life, which Paul teaches in Romans 8: the presence of the love and joy of God, and the overwhelming sense of longing and yearning and of 'not yet'. When he teaches beginners he is very keen to emphasise these two aspects. 'When you start to pray the Jesus prayer, I urge people now to say, "I want to want the presence and love of God in Christ." The intention is not to say the prayer but to allow the Lord to draw you into His presence through the power of the Holy Spirit.'

Not only is Bishop Simon soaked in the Bible, but he lives the prayer, rather than just teaching about it at a theoretical level. This gives him a deep authenticity and lends an attractiveness to his words as he speaks to me. 'The yearning comes from Jesus. He ever lives to make intercession for us. And we sense our interceding is joining us with Him. There is that sense that there is a longing in heaven for the wholeness of God's love to enfold us.'

For Bishop Simon, the name of Jesus is very precious and powerful. He makes the point that there is a great emphasis on the name of Jesus in the New Testament, that His name is His real nature.

As I speak to Bishop Simon I have the sense that he really believes the Jesus Prayer could have huge significance for the church in the world, and that it should not be seen as something esoteric and strange. He has used it with beginners, and those seeking to go deeper into prayer. He has taught it to those lying immobilised in hospital. It is simple enough for anyone to pray, and has evangelistic potential with those interested in New Spirituality (formerly known as the New Age movement).

In the introduction to the new edition of his book, he also writes of the connection he believes there could be between this unceasing prayer and the 24-7 prayer movement started by Pete Greig.

At the end he comes back to the Desert Fathers who drew people to them, and then sent them back into the world to change it. 'The martyrs had been the great inspiration previously, and the Desert Fathers became their successors at inspiring people to transform the world. It is interesting that in this period the prayer was at its strongest, love was at its greatest. "See how these Christians love one another," was being said, and people were drawn into the kingdom in unprecedented numbers.'

As I talk to him I have the sense that this is one of the most important things he has been given to do – to teach this prayer to as wide an audience as possible.

One of his maxims is that a sermon without the love of God is not worth preaching.

As he speaks, I am increasingly aware this prayer has the power to scatter the fear of death, to scatter anxiety.

Day 25: Getting real with happiness

We need a new perspective on happiness, and I want to give us one here. In psychology, for every 100 studies on depression there is one study on happiness. However, there is a new interest in researching happiness, both in the world of psychology and in the Christian world.

As Christians, the first hurdle to overcome is actually to believe that God wants us to be happy. Pollyanna tells us in the film of the same name that there are 826 glad texts in the Bible, and if God goes to the trouble to tell us to be happy that many times, we should pay attention.

Of course, 'happiness' is a much misunderstood word. In Psalm 16:11 we read:

> You have made known to me the path of life;
> you will fill me with joy in your presence,
> with eternal pleasures at your right hand.

True happiness is to be found in God's presence, which is a gift of grace as well as something we experience when we are pure in heart (Matthew 5:8). How to become pure in heart is another story.

We often think that happiness is only to be experienced in temporary ways. But that is to confuse happiness for momentary pleasures such as eating a bar of chocolate.

There are things that bring us enduring happiness. Many more married people say they are very happy than single people, despite the bad press wedlock gets these days.

One professor in the United States began his career investigating disgust.[50] One of his tests was to give people

---

[50] Quoted in Martin E. P. Seligman, *Authentic Happiness* (London: Nicholas Brealey Publishing, 2003) p.8.

fried grasshoppers to eat. When he wanted to measure moral disgust he gave people a shirt to wear that was apparently worn by Adolf Hitler. In the end, fed up with measuring negative feelings, he tried to work out if there was a positive feeling which was the opposite of moral disgust.

He discovered something he called 'elevation'. Apparently, when we see somebody doing something extraordinarily kind for someone else, or we do something good for someone else, we can feel this sense of elevation, which is a form of happiness, and is not to be confused with pride.

Another interesting piece of research on happiness is that most people operate within set parameters of happiness, ranging from the pessimistic to the optimistic. Twenty-three people who had won the lottery were followed up in terms of their levels of happiness. After the initial euphoria of winning millions had worn off, those winners, without exception, fell back to their previous set levels of happiness. So money does not make us happy in the way we might expect it to.

Scientists didn't think that people could move out of these set levels of happiness, but that view is now changing. In Christian terms, when Peter talks about a joy that is inexpressible and glorious (1 Peter 1:8), and we experience a peace that is beyond human understanding, we have long affirmed that our levels of happiness are not determined by our genes or our circumstances.

It was Gandhi who apparently said:

I like your Christ, I do not like your Christians. Your Christians are so unlike your Christ.

Jesus of Nazareth was the most joyous being to walk the earth, and our reputation as Christians is very often that of righteously mean people who think it is more important to be right than loving.

Psalm 4:6–7 says:

127

Many are asking, 'Who can show us any good?'
Let the light of our face shine upon us, O Lord.
You have filled my heart with greater joy
Than when their grain and new wine abound.

Again, we are reminded about the happiness that comes from being in God's presence, which is greater than that gained by an abundance of material possessions. If people in the world could see Christians exhibiting that authentic happiness in the midst of difficult economic circumstances, I am sure the queues that used to be outside the Next sales would transfer to churches.

Another interesting bit of research suggests that happiness is infectious and rubs off on others. I am sure that is also true of misery. If we truly have the path of life that brings joy and happiness, then now is the time to allow that happiness to radiate through our relationships. Perhaps the greater part of being contagiously holy, as Jesus was, is to be contagiously happy.

As you read Mark's gospel over the next few days, ask yourself what it might say about happiness, and ask what is your relationship to happiness. I have been thinking recently about my relationship with it.

The boy on the edge of happiness is the title of a book of poetry by Matthew Hollis.[51] I haven't read the book, or what I am imagining to be a poem of the same name, but I came across Hollis and looked him up. That's when the title, 'The boy on the edge of happiness' resonated deeply. It brought into my awareness something that was on the edge of my awareness: as a boy and as a man I have lived on the edge of happiness. Why would anyone do that?

---

[51] Matthew Hollis, *The Boy on the Edge of Happiness* (Smith Doorstep, 1996).

I have known happiness, and at crucial times in my life it felt like it was taken away. So I never quite trusted it to stay around. The first time was when I went to boarding school at the age of six and three-quarters, for a term. We would have a day sometime during the term when our parents would take us out, called an exeat. At the beginning of the day happiness would flood back. My mum says I would chat to them, and be lively and excited. But as the day drew to a close I would be quiet and would not speak; I would just look at them with my eyes filling with tears, but without crying. Happiness was draining away, or being taken away.

In short, happiness couldn't be trusted; it was safer to live on the edge of happiness.

I remember, when I was a little older, my brother and I would fly home to Kenya for the holidays from the UK from another school. The first night in my bedroom in Kenya would be a strange one. I would wake up on the first morning of the holidays, as light streamed through the curtains, with a sinking heart as I imagined I was still at school. Suddenly I would realise this was a different sort of light and I would be filled with a sense of elation – I was home.

The first night at boarding school reversed the process. I would awake imagining I was home, with a light heart, and then realise with a sinking feeling that I was back at school.

The title of Matthew Hollis' book of poetry rang me like a bell. I was filled with the revelation that ever since those early experiences I had lived on the edge of happiness. I would never quite allow myself to enter in all its fullness the happiness that was there, in case it was taken away.

The reason for writing about these memories that came back was that I wondered how many other people are living quietly on the edge of happiness for similar reasons?

When my mum told me the story of the exeat she said it used to break her heart to have to let me go back to the boarding part of school. The title of a poem has given me a deep mindful insight. Poetry has this capacity.

I am experimenting, right now, mindfully, with trying to enter into the full experience of happiness, moment by moment as it arises. I felt it today. A moment of happiness should not be dismissed.

There is a whole world in a single moment. Even a world of happiness.

Day 26: Correcting the distortion of superiority

We might not talk so much these days about upper class, middle class or lower class, but we still play the everyday games of upperness and lowerness. We still say, 'I've got the upper hand', 'he's an upstart', 'she needs pulling down a peg or two', 'back down', 'she looked down her nose', and we play the games of one-upmanship, keeping up appearances, and so on. It's a game the disciples played in Mark (9:34), when they argued about who was the greatest.

The apostle Peter's vision in Joppa made him realise that he could not maintain his assumed position of religious superiority over Gentiles. He said, 'I now realise how true it is that God does not show favouritism but accepts men from every nation who fear him and do what is right' (Acts 10:34–35).

Even early on in Mark's gospel the religious leaders keep their distance from Jesus and the kingdom. It appears that they believe they are superior, and that they believe their control over the religious system is threatened by Jesus. This results in them having a critical and judgemental spirit.

With Mark's gospel in your hand, read about the healing of the paralytic at the beginning of chapter 2, and the reaction of the religious leaders. As they sit there in a judgemental and critical way, there is an implication that they are keeping their distance. A religious leader who is one of the minor characters helps illuminate this for us. Read Mark 12:28–34 and reflect on what Jesus says to the teacher of the law.

Jesus says to him, 'You are not far from the kingdom of God' (Mark 12:34). The teacher is not far from the kingdom of God and his answer to Jesus has the seeds of kingdom awareness within it. As we keep our distance we remain outsiders, without awareness, unable to pay attention to what is there below the surface. As we come near to the right place (and we need to ask ourselves what is that place in Mark) then we are given revelation and can become more attentive to God's reality.

If instead of humility we have an attitude of being superior and right, then we won't approach Jesus and ask for His transforming help – because we believe we are just fine as we are.

This attitude of critical superiority can spill into all our relationships, including marriage. Very often conflict ceases to be about issues but becomes about criticising the other person. The emotion that underlines the personal character assassination that goes on is contempt – we have contempt for people we think are not as important as we are. Without necessarily being fully aware of it, we believe the person we once loved is stupid, selfish, a fool.

Those in the helping professions are not immune. There is a lot of evidence for the existence of 'therapeutic disdain' shown towards people with learning difficulties.

Many of the conflicts in church, whatever theological language they are dressed up in, are battles between different groups trying to maintain their position of power and control, out of assumed superiority.

How do we avoid the terrible games of 'Who is the greatest?' and 'I want to get my own way because I am right and superior, and you are below me because you are stupid and useless'?

We start by looking at ourselves. We need to start making humility in its true sense the heart of our personal and corporate lives. Humility, as Abbot Christopher Jamison says in his book *Finding Sanctuary*, is not insincere grovelling; it is not passive, meek behaviour, it is not just for introverts and little old ladies – it is for all of us.

Humility from its root word *humus* means being down to earth, knowing our strengths and weaknesses. It is false humility that says, 'I don't have any strengths', and false pride that won't admit to weaknesses. Humility recognises that we are all equal.

Abbot Christopher says that each human being plays out the story of Adam and Eve, where people 'struggle to be down-to-earth and avoid the temptation to act as if they were the divine centre of the universe'.[52]

Humility, above all, is a community virtue – the rule of St Benedict says that part of humility is 'that a man loves not his own will'.[53]

If we truly know that we are equal, that we are made in the image of God, then we don't need to sustain this false position of assumed superiority to bolster our egos. If we know our strengths and weaknesses as God's children we won't constantly need to seek our own way or personal advantage. We can begin to serve instead of seeking to be served.

This humility is shown to us throughout Mark's gospel. It is implied as a value for discipleship. As Jesus said to the disciples when they were arguing about who was the greatest (who was superior), 'If anyone wants to be first, he must be the very last, and the servant of all' (Mark 9:35). This humility requires true ethical mindfulness.

---

[52] Abbot Christopher Jamison, *Finding Sanctuary*, p.85.
[53] Timothy Fry (Ed.), *The Rule of St. Benedict in English* (Collegeville/ Minnesota: The Liturgical Press, 1982) p.34.

Day 27: Repairing our face-to-face relationships through compassion

In various mindfulness approaches there are befriending or compassion meditations. These again have their roots in Buddhist tradition of *metta*, or loving-kindness meditations. These would include compassion for oneself, a stranger and even someone we find difficult.

Of course, loving-kindness and compassion play a central part in Christianity as well. As I looked at these *metta* meditations I was struck by their similarity to the prayer of Ananias of Damascus for Saul of Tarsus.

In chapter nine of the Book of Acts in the New Testament, Saul has his famous Damascus Road experience. He is on his way to Damascus to arrest followers of The Way (Christians) when he is arrested by the risen Lord Jesus Christ.

Temporarily blinded, Saul is led into Damascus. A man there called Ananias has a vision from God who asks him to go and pray a prayer of blessing on Saul which will restore his sight and fill him with the compassionate presence of God, the Holy Spirit.

Ananias questions the wisdom of praying for a stranger and an enemy, but God encourages him out of the way of fear into the way of love. It is clear that the prayer of Ananias has a significant impact on Saul. When Saul talks about his encounter with Jesus, which includes the prayer of Ananias when scales fell from his eyes and he is filled with the Holy Spirit, he says he has had three important experiences.

'Not that I have already obtained all this, or have already been made perfect, but I press on to take hold of that for which Christ Jesus took hold of me' (Philippians 3:12). The word here for 'took hold' is literally 'arrested'. On the road to Damascus the love of Christ took hold of him.

When the scales fell from his eyes he 'saw the light'. In 2 Corinthians 4:6 he says:

> For God, who said, 'Let light shine out of darkness,' made his light shine in our hearts to give us the light of the knowledge of the glory of God in the face of Christ.

This reference to light shining out of darkness goes back to Genesis 1:3 where God said, 'Let there be light.'

So Saul was taken hold of by the love of Christ, and the light of the love of God shone in his heart.

He then says in 1 Timothy 1:13–14:

> Even though I was once a blasphemer and a persecutor and a violent man, I was shown mercy because I acted in ignorance and unbelief. The grace of our Lord was poured out on me abundantly, along with the faith and love that are in Christ Jesus.

The compassionate mercy, grace and love of God were poured into Paul like an overwhelming river.

I felt in part that these experiences were because of Ananias' prayer of befriending and compassion. So I have put them in prayer form that we can pray first for ourselves, then for a stranger, then for an enemy, and finally for ourselves again. The words of one of Jesus' most important statements are, 'Love your neighbour as yourself' (Matthew 22:39).

These are the prayers:

> May the love of Christ take hold of me;
> May the light of Christ shine in my heart;
> May the love of Christ flow through me like a river.

and then:

May the love of Christ take hold of him/her;
May the light of Christ shine in his/her heart;
May the love of Christ flow through him/her like a river.

We pray it for our own self, then for a stranger, then for an enemy, and finally for our own self again. Change is laid down by a succession of fresh experiences of love. In our prayer of blessing and befriending, something real happens. It enables face-to-face meetings to be more holistically relational. It also enables us to face within ourselves parts of ourselves that we don't like, or that we think God might not like. It also enables us to face those whom we find difficult or who might be angry with us, or even hate us.

Day 28: New ...

As we move towards the climax of the gospel, I want you to read three passages: Mark 3:20–35; Mark 10:29–31; Mark 13:33–36. Ask yourself what they have in common.

In Mark 3:20–35 we have a Markan sandwich: two stories about Jesus and His natural family, with a conflict with the religious leaders in between. The stories about Jesus and His family have caused controversy, and endless debates about what they might mean. How do these verses make you feel?

One of the possibilities is to not try and explain the embarrassment of Jesus' family being in conflict with Him, but to allow it to be a bit of grit that produces the pearl of new thinking. Perhaps it is an exegetical riddle that we can never solve, but that can produce new thinking. The other major challenge is that our new family in Christ may lead us into conflict with our natural family, and that our natural family doesn't have priority automatically.

There are other verbal echoes here. The word 'house' (*oikon*) is an important repetition in Mark's gospel. Scholars believe the gospel began life as an oral performance which would have been performed as a whole piece. Those listening would have picked up on the repeated different verbal echoes that Mark uses.

In Mark 1:29 we are told that Jesus goes to the house of Simon and Andrew. He visits the same house in Mark 2:1, and it seems it has become a 'home' to Him. The passage as a whole in Mark 3:20–35 is full of household and family imagery. Mark is telling us the importance of meeting in community, and the shocking importance of that new community. Jesus says, 'Whoever does God's will is my brother and sister and mother' (Mark 3:35).

It is not that you abandon your family, but that they might leave you. Above all, it is about when the natural family becomes an idol, or wants us to conform to outward forms of behaviour (Mark 3:21). It is also about recognition that the things we think are rock solid often are not.

It is not about duty but implicitly about a desire to do God's will. When the disciples follow Jesus immediately (Mark 1:18) we are given no rational explanation, but again perhaps it is to do with spiritual desire.

Household language reappears in the section that is sandwiched by the two aspects of the story of Jesus' family. Jesus ties up the strong man, that is Satan, so that he can enter his house and 'carry off his possessions' (Mark 3:27). Jesus carries out His exorcisms through the power of the Holy Spirit, but He is accused by the teachers of the law of carrying it out through an evil spirit (Mark 3:30). Yet again there is misunderstanding, a failure to see or hear truly what is shown to us through the gospel. This distorted interpreting of reality is one of the fundamental fault lines within us that needs healing. So strongly does Jesus believe this that when Peter misunderstands His Passion prediction, He says to Peter, 'Out of my sight, Satan!' (Mark 8:33).

Augustine says something similar when he defines the nature of evil within us as 'the perversion of my capacity to see or know'.[54] This mis-seeing needs to be transformed into true seeing. To be aware of this mis-seeing is to be truly mindful in a Christian sense, as is to be aware of the possibility of transformation through Christ.

We begin to see truly when we put ourselves in the place of the servant. In Mark 10:44 we must be the *diakonos*, the household servant. In Week Five we will come on to the key

[54] Rowan Williams, 'Insubstantial Evil' in *Augustine and his Critics: Essays in Honour of Gerald Bonner,* edited by Robert Dodaro & George Lawless (London: Routledge, 2000) p.107.

passages in Mark 13 and 14 on discernment and watchfulness. One of the key sections in these passages is Mark 13:33–37, where servants are put in charge of the 'house'. Through repetition we realise that this ordinary word 'house' begins to signify something else, to point to a greater reality.

Week Five

Day 29: Opening our awareness

Read Mark 13 and 14 this week. Check your reading – are you reading aggressively or are you reading slowly and mindfully?

As we look again at watchfulness, there is an element of yearning and desire within it. *Lectio Divina* helps us to enter into that yearning. Michael Casey OCSO, a leading monastic writer on *Lectio*, says that part of this form of reading is the anagogical sense of reading Scripture, as defined by the mediaeval theologians. That is, real things in the Bible point to a greater reality. This sense, he says, teaches us spiritual desire, which he calls the engine of spiritual progress.[55] This anagogical sense has also been called parabolic, and so Mark's gospel in particular, as a parabolic piece of writing, lends itself to this way of reading Scripture.

The disciples in Mark show positive qualities as well as an astonishing lack of understanding. They do 'follow', and this is to do with desire, which is inchoate. The rich man who ran to Jesus and fell on his knees, in a society where men did not run, is showing spiritual desire (Mark 10:17). His desire for his wealth, however, wins the wrestling match (Mark 10:22).

Mark 13:33–37 is a summary parable; it has also been called a parable of crisis. It begins with the imperative *blepete*, literally 'look', or often translated 'be on guard'. This word 'look' or 'see' has been used as a verbal thread throughout the

---

[55] 'Make My *Word* your Home: An exploration of *Lectio Divina*', seven talks recorded at Worth Abbey, 15-17th July 2009.

gospel. This is particularly obvious in the Greek, and in the original oral performances of the gospel. It is followed by the crisis in the Garden of Gethsemane and the crisis of the arrest, trial and crucifixion.

Earlier key repetitions include Mark 4:12, 24; 5:31; 8:15, 18, 23, 24; 12:14, 38. You might want to look these up. It is in the repetition that we realise that Mark is giving this word a greater meaning than its literal meaning. It is a focused attention, much like the anagogical sensing of Scripture that enables us to see through the visible to the invisible, but with a narrow concentrated focus – and an ability to diagnose or discern.

'Watch out (*blepete*) for the yeast of the Pharisees and that of Herod,' (Mark 8:15) says Jesus.

In the parable, Mark then switches to his other key word *gregoreo*, usually translated 'watch'. Here he uses it three times (Mark 13:34, 35, 37). This is a more open awareness that leads to insight and true seeing. This word foreshadows its use in Mark 14:32–42 in the Garden of Gethsemane scene. Perhaps the garden scene is another enacted parable where Jesus models true discipleship as watchfulness. The disciples themselves fail to be watchful. What they are to watch is the eschatological crisis that is to follow – the death and resurrection of Jesus. 'The hour has come. Look, the Son of Man is betrayed into the hands of sinners', says Jesus.

The disciples have already stumbled at the cross, earlier in Mark – each time Jesus makes His Passion predictions, which He does three times (Mark 8:31; 9:31; 10:33). The watching He calls them to is not a fearful watching which is about the saving of self, as in Mark 4:35–40 where they wake a 'sleeping' Jesus. (This is a fear that is not appropriate, unlike the fear connected with the many epiphanies in Mark which is appropriate.) They are to be wakeful, as Jesus is the Wakeful One.

What they are to watch is another place – what happens on the cross. The women attentively watch the cross from a distance (Mark 15:40). The cross itself is parabolic – it has a deeper reality that they are called to see. This is the place of true revelation. Mark has already told us what that meaning is – 'For even the Son of Man did not come to be served, but to serve, and to give his life as a ransom for many' (Mark 10:45). Jesus took our place on the cross that we might take His place in the kingdom of His Father. It is at the foot of the cross that all disciples need to be watchful, because that is where we will find the fullest revelation, and the authority (Mark 13:34) that enables us to shift our allegiance from the things of the world to the things of God. In that place we find freedom from the slaveries that lead us astray in the world.

The cross opens our awareness to aspects of ourselves and the world that we would rather avoid as we focus attention on it. It offers freedom, not more chains of slavery.

Day 30: Working with neuroscience and cognitive psychology

I mentioned earlier the overlapping concepts in psychological science and Buddhism of present-moment awareness and mindfulness. One of the key points of watchfulness is what it does for us.

I come across so many people who seem unable to shift their moods. They are stuck in depression, anxiety, anger or bitterness. The slightest shift in circumstances sends them into a negative downward spiral. I'm not saying this to judge, but out of love.

What is interesting about the lament psalms is the psalmist's ability to shift his mood. Psalm 13 begins with the words, 'How long, O Lord? Will you forget me for ever?' and ends five verses later, 'I will sing to the Lord, for he has been good to me.' It seems that a process is followed which brings an awareness that enables this shift of mood from despair to joy, turmoil to peace.

In Psalm 1 the psalmist outlines that process: 'on his law he meditates day and night' (verse 2). This sustains him, in the same way a tree is sustained when planted by water. The simple truth is that when we are stuck in a negative mood, automatic and distorted thoughts run our lives out of our awareness.

In the process of meditating on Scripture, we find our minds wandering. We find it hard and tiring work to drag attention away from ourselves. Indeed, the minute we relax, our mind, like an elastic band being stretched, snaps back to our own selfish concerns. If we pay attention to what has dragged our attention away from Scripture, we find that automatic and distorted thoughts are responsible.

We know that Romans 12:2 says, 'Do not conform any longer to the pattern of this world, but be transformed by the renewing of your mind.' One of the ways this is possible is through meditation on Scripture. One of the cognitive steps we need to take in the renewing of our minds is, as we have said, to 'take captive every thought to make it obedient to Christ' (2 Corinthians 10:5).

We can't take any thoughts captive until we become aware of the automatic distorted ones that secretly run our lives. The whole process of meditation enables this awareness.

Now if we can take our thoughts captive, and if, as in Psalm 13, we can wrestle with our thoughts – what does that say about the relationship between us and our thoughts? It means we are not our thoughts. Our minds are a bigger container than our thoughts.

If we assume we are our thoughts – for example, 'I am always going to be unhappy' – we will be unhappy. If we can take that thought captive by saying, 'I am not my thoughts,' that thought will begin to fade away, as a cloud disappears in the sky once the sun shines. This is the central insight of mindfulness, whether Christian, secular or Buddhist (but I am giving this insight a Christian scaffolding here). Through this insight we begin to find inner freedom.

Romans 8:6 says that 'to be spiritually minded is life and peace' (KJV). There is a measurable shift in our mood – life and peace are real things we can experience. We can use the word 'awareness' to talk about this spiritually minded life, or we could use the word 'mindfulness'.

Psalm 8:4 says, 'What is man that you are mindful of him?' To be mindful in the Hebrew, apparently, is not just to remember; it is to express concern, to act with loving care.

Peter writes his second letter 'That ye may be mindful of the words which were spoken before by the holy prophets...'

(3:2 KJV). To be mindful, to practise mindfulness, is more than just remembering.

There are some words that we need to begin using again, like the tenderness of 'thou' compared to the impersonal 'you'. 'Mindful' is just such a word.

Mindfulness as a word, concept and process is big news within the counselling world. There is a new wave of therapy that combines mindfulness with cognitive behavioural therapy. Research shows that mindfulness can significantly transform a person suffering from mood disorders.

Mindfulness in this new wave of therapy comes from practising meditative techniques originating in Buddhism. These techniques, like focusing on your breath, appear to be neutral – they do not involve emptying your mind or invoking any unknown spiritual forces. No particular religion owns the breath, and Christianity has its own theology of the breath. The techniques involve becoming fully alert to our thoughts, our feelings and what is going on inside our bodies. There is more work to be done in the psychological sciences in researching this phenomenon, but that is happening. Mindfulness for health is a very important development within secular psychology

However, mindfulness is not just a Buddhist concept, nor is it an aspect of secular psychology; it is a universal human capacity. It can be accessed in many ways, by artists, poets, carpenters, fishermen, ballet dancers, children. These are earthed, reality-focused pursuits.

Within our own Christian tradition, ancient meditative practices and forms of contemplative prayer create a state of awareness, or mindfulness – but this is not often talked about. Within the Christian tradition I would call it 'mind*Full*ness', as we cannot empty our minds, although we can still them – and we are aware of the dimension of God's divine presence working within us.

Instead of doing the evangelical swoon the minute words like 'meditation' and 'mindfulness' are used, we need to start exploring and practising contemplative prayer in all its rich variety. We also need to enter into a creative dialogue with mindfulness and mental health issues.

Also, if we are to witness with credibility to our Hindu and Buddhist neighbours, we need to be able to find common ground in this whole area of meditation. There is a way to golden moments and brighter days and living springs, for us and for others. Let's be mindful of it.

Day 31: The Jesus Prayer – the heart of the spiritual relationship

When I began to use the Jesus Prayer it acted very like some of the Celtic prayers, as a circle of protection. For a while it kept at bay the feelings of anxiety or the afflictive thoughts that were troubling me. But if you read the writings of the Desert Fathers and Mothers you find out there are some thoughts (and in the end all thoughts) that you can't keep at bay. They called these the Eight Afflictive Thoughts, which became trivialised as the Seven Deadly Sins.

These were pride, anger, lust, gluttony, acedia, sadness, greed and vanity. At some point, as these thoughts are kept at bay for a while, we realise that we are not our thoughts, that we are bigger than our thoughts. If we are aware that we can take them captive, that relativises them – they are smaller and less powerful than we think. They are not the powers and authorities that they can become in our minds. By characterising these afflictive thoughts as demons, the Desert Fathers and Mothers achieved this observing distance from their thoughts; they relativised them in that way. This is mindfulness at work.

Mark tells us that one of the reasons we fail to see and hear and understand the mystery of the kingdom, the key to real living, is that we have hard hearts. Jesus asks the disciples, 'Are your hearts hardened?' (Mark 8:17) when they fail to understand the feeding of the 5,000. Contemplative practices like *Lectio Divina* and the Jesus Prayer enable us to open and soften our hearts – that is why they are so applicable to helping us become the disciples Mark wants us to be.

At some point we have to move from the Jesus Prayer acting like a protective circle, to something more like a fragile coracle in which we enter the sea of our thoughts and feelings and the wider world and God. We move out of the harbour into the open sea. The harbour is the place of experiential avoidance; the sea is where we engage with what we have been hiding from, what we have run from, what we have pushed down out of our awareness. We move from a place of narrow concentration to a place of open awareness.

We move from avoiding our difficult experiences to facing the reality of them – again, this is the heart of being mindful. We are exposed to what is really going on inside us. This can be very painful, and so we often also avoid contemplative or mindful practices, and we often avoid silence and solitude so that we don't have to face our inner struggles.

From a psychological perspective, the disciples in Mark are guilty of experiential avoidance. When Jesus talks about the way of the cross and predicts His Passion, Peter rebukes Him (Mark 8:32). He has to remind them twice more, in Mark 9 and 10, and then again in chapters 13 and 14. Watchfulness is facing reality, not running away from it, or pretending something else is reality – like being the greatest, saving one's self, or gaining the whole world.

Experiential avoidance is a psychological process that seeks to avoid what we believe will be painful feelings, thoughts, memories and bodily sensations within us. It causes us problems psychologically. For example, in times of conflict I would avoid facing the experience of my anger. I would end up with very tight neck and shoulder muscles that could go into spasm. But when I faced the anger and the cluster of thoughts, feelings and bodily sensations with it, the anger did not seem to be such a fearful power and authority as I thought it was.

I have often tried to avoid anxious feelings by keeping busy. But as the Jesus Prayer helps us to slow down and still ourselves, we become aware of what we have been avoiding.

This is using the Jesus Prayer mindfully, as those who used it to face the eight afflictive thoughts used it mindfully.

How do we begin with the Jesus Prayer? It is important to pay attention to the body. Posture is important, and the way we sit. I find a prayer stool or a straight-backed chair where one can sit relaxed but in a good frame is important. Where we sit is also very important. Choose a place you can return to again and again that has no distractions. We can also pray the Jesus Prayer walking somewhere, or out in the world doing something else.

Traditionally in the Jesus Prayer, the first half of the sentence is prayed on the in-breath – 'Lord Jesus Christ, Son of God,' – and the second half of the sentence is prayed on the out-breath – 'have mercy on me, a sinner.' The breath is neutral; it belongs to no particular religious group. Breathing is something we all do, and we take it with us wherever we go. That makes it a useful aid in our prayer life. When we are anxious we often over-breathe, and this rhythmic use of it in the Jesus Prayer slows our breathing down.

I find that I repeat the prayer in cycles of 25, with a pause in between the cycles to offer prayers for whatever comes to mind, or simply to be in open awareness or contemplation of God's presence. Beginning with four cycles is a good start.

It takes time to learn to move out of the harbour of experiential avoidance into the open sea, in the coracle of the simple prayer. In Mark's gospel we are made aware of our incompleteness and need to be open to God at all times. The Jesus Prayer brings us to that point as well. Mark's gospel teaches us perseverance – what has been called 'deep practice'. Those who master a craft are distinguished by how much time they spend in practice, not by their innate ability. A concert pianist will have done on average 10,000 hours of practice to arrive at that level of skill. The Jesus Prayer reminds us about the need for 'deep practice'. However, God in His grace may give us moments of epiphany that keep us praying in this way.

Day 32: Getting more real with happiness

Mark's gospel gives us an implied perspective on happiness, but it is not what we might expect. We need to look at our own expectations as well. Human beings find it very difficult to be happy. We are distracted by pleasures that bring momentary happiness, and lose sight of the things that would bring us enduring happiness.

In part, our happiness depends on what we do with the past. Pastors and theologians have known this for a long time. One of the main tools for breaking up the bitter soil of a resentfully remembered past is forgiveness.

Until recently, psychologists have dismissed forgiveness as something that should be embalmed and put in the museum along with other religious relics. However, they are now beginning to change their minds. But can we scatter the seeds of forgiveness as open-handedly as Jesus asks us to?

When Peter says to Jesus (Matthew 18:21), 'How many times shall I forgive my brother when he sins against me? Up to seven times?' he is being generous by rabbinic standards of the day. Forgiving someone up to three times was the standard answer. Most commentators suggest that Jesus' reply, 'seventy-seven times' or 'seventy times seven', means that we are to forgive without number, an infinite number of times.

Surely this is just asking other people to walk all over us, to use us as a doormat, to take advantage? At the heart of the parable is the realisation that we are to forgive as God forgives us, with the same measure, and His forgiveness is extravagant and infinite.

Why is this? It is because to God, forgiveness is part of His covenant of committed relationship of love with us. One of the greatest such expressions of covenant love which mirrors God's love for us is Ruth's words to Naomi:

> Where you go I will go, and where you stay I will stay. Your people will be my people and your God my God.
> *Ruth 1:16*

William Nicholson, who wrote the screenplays for *Shadowlands* and *Gladiator*, takes these words in his trilogy for children, *The Wind on Fire*, and translates them beautifully into vows for marriage, as well as for living in community:

> Where you go, I go. Where you stay, I stay. When you sleep, I will sleep. When you rise, I will rise. I will pass my days within the sound of your voice, and my nights within the reach of your hand. And none shall come between us.[56]

On the cross, Jesus extends the hand of God in forgiveness to us and His death says to us, 'and none shall come between us, and nothing shall come between us'. When we extend the hand of forgiveness to others again and again, we are saying, 'and none shall come between us, and nothing shall come between us'.

With God there is always the chance for a new beginning. Despite the many failures of the disciples in Mark's gospel, at the end the angel says to the women in words of beginning again:

> But go, tell his disciples and Peter, 'He is going ahead of you into Galilee. There you will see him, just as he told you.'
> *Mark 16:7*

---

[56] William Nicholson, *Firesong* (London: Egmont, 2002) p.340.

Forgiveness enables us to begin again. The bindweed that chokes happiness in the present is bitterness and vengeful anger about the past, a refusal to forgive.

It is not just that we risk depression by dwelling on past wrongs; the poison of anger and bitterness work their way into our bodies and damage our physical health. In popular culture we are still enamoured of a Freudian view of emotional hydraulics – that we need to express our emotions, especially anger, as if they are contained within an impermeable membrane.

The latest research on emotions suggests that our feelings will leak away by a process of emotional osmosis if we allow them to, allowing our mood to settle back into whatever our set range is. In a study of medical students over 25 years, the angriest students had five times as much heart disease as the least angry ones. It is the overt expression of anger that is dangerous.

It is not only that we over-emphasise the bad things that have happened to us in the past; we can also fail to appreciate enough the good things that have happened. Apparently, when we intentionally go out of our way to express gratitude for the good things in our lives, levels of happiness jump significantly.

Receiving the expression of somebody's authentic gratitude is also beneficial to our levels of happiness, if, in our cultural restrictions, we can allow ourselves to savour such expressions of love without shrinking with embarrassment.

If in the next week every Christian in the country expressed authentic gratitude to someone else, who knows what that ripple of appreciation might do? If we expressed authentic gratitude for the life given as a ransom for us, what might be possible in transforming the world and serving as we have been served?

Let's be golden-hearted with our thanks and gratitude and mine some gold of happiness from the soil of the past.

Day 33: Repairing our vision

Very few people can make you feel pure, special and extraordinary. Very few make you feel you are the right person with the right human face. Jesus had that capacity. On the resurrection morning, the eighth day of creation, He said Mary's name with love, and she was transformed with a radiance of joy (John 20:16).

She would have danced with the sun, leapt over roofs and trees. It is in that elemental change of the wild creation of God we find true happiness.

The problem is, we have had another world pulled over our eyes. We have been wrapped up in the great embrace of consumerism promising endless joy but consuming us from the inside out.

We are promised that our problems will Vanish in the land of Plenty. The Auto will provide the Emocion we lack. The walk of shame will end with a bottle of vitamin water. We will be made clean by Listerine. We will be made magnetically attractive by the Lynx bullet. These are religious claims of fullness in a land of emptiness. In their own way they are as baneful as the big lies of communist propaganda.

These 24/7 whispers and visual fragments stop us hearing and seeing the one Voice who can lead us back into the real world.

We perceive this world of the Great Embrace with its black and white fallacies, appeals to greed and vanity, full of beautiful people, half-truths and glittering generalities as real. We need to see it as it really is – an elaborate deception designed to keep us docile and usable as sources of energy for the intelligent machine of selfish capitalism.

We need to believe as literal truth what the One said, that we are slaves to sin (John 8:34). We need to believe that we need ransoming (Mark 10:45) from the slave market. One of the most eye-opening visual representations of this slavery is the 1999 Wachowski brothers film *The Matrix*.

In the film, human beings are farmed in individual vats of nutrients while their body heat is used as a source of energy by sentient machines. The human beings are kept conformed and docile by their minds being plugged into a virtual-simulated construct patterned on the real world; it is called the Matrix.

Some humans have found freedom, unplugged themselves and cleansed the doors of their perception, aware that something is wrong. They are seeking to rescue others, including someone called Neo. They believe he is the one to set them free.

Once free, the resistance fighters plug back into the system, but this time they know it is an illusion. At one point, when Neo realises who he truly is, he is able to see the Matrix for what it really is – a stream of green computer coding, and that pattern of coding, the digital rain, suddenly falls to a new pattern.

We are told, 'Do not conform any longer to the pattern of this world, but be transformed by the renewing of your mind' (Romans 12:2).

The patterns of this world in our minds are like computer coding that enslave and control us. Once we let the One into our minds, into the system, then the pattern begins to be renewed, begins to change. Something really is rewritten inside us; there is a new stream of consciousness.

I have tried to represent this in a painting, where the new words are the living words of God, and they stream through our minds as new coding, bringing freedom and release from slavery. In the painting I have used key words and phrases in Greek from the New Testament: Jesus Christ Son of God,

Spirit-Bearers, disciple – representing what we are to become, and the one who is to transform our becoming.

But first we need to realise something is wrong, that we are slaves, in a prison we cannot smell or taste or touch.

There are many who will not be told that this is the truth, just as they cannot accept that there is another reality. We have to try and help them walk through the door, into the wardrobe, down the rabbit hole, into the painting.

Then we can truly say, 'Welcome to the real world.' The world of true happiness where Jesus helps us fall awake, brings us fully alive, to the glory of God.

Day 34: The kingdom awakening

Gillian Ayres, the British abstract painter, created a picture recently called *The Seeds that Woke the Clay*. At the beginning of the Bible we have the breath that awoke the clay. In Mark's gospel we have the seed of the kingdom that grows secretly and mysteriously (4:27). In the same way that seed awakes – this is the hidden message of Mark's focus on the disciples' inability to see or to hear or to understand clearly – we need the kingdom awakening.

This helps shed light on the nature of revelation in Mark. There is a universal human capacity for awareness and attention that we can develop, but there is a deeper awakening that is a gift from God. The seed of the kingdom awakens the understanding, but revelation is also in the gift and freedom of God.

There is a new dimension to revelation in Mark's gospel, which begins with Jesus seeing 'heaven being torn open' (Mark 1:10). The same word is used at the end of the gospel when after Jesus' death the curtain of the Temple was torn in two (Mark 15:38).

Intriguingly, not only is the kingdom of God near (Mark 1:15) but there are mysterious doors in Mark 13:29 (*thurais*). The watchers in the parable of crisis (Mark 13:33–37) are to be doorkeepers (*thururo*). The doorkeeper is to be near the door of the kingdom. In fact, Lightfoot translates the phrase in Mark 1:15 as 'the kingdom of God is at the doors'.[57]

What brings us near the doors is when we find the place of courage and of risking ourselves for others rather than the fearful saving of self. When the Temple curtain is torn in two,

---

[57] R. H. Lightfoot, *The Gospel Message of St Mark* (London: OUP, 1950) p.20.

the presence which remakes the clay – the presence of God – moves from the inmost place of the Temple to the new holiest place – the cross of Jesus. This is the place where a Gentile centurion says, 'Surely this man was the Son of God' (Mark 15:39).

When we stand at the foot of the cross, we are in the place where the doors of the kingdom are fully open. When we stand in the place of the presence of God that remakes the clay, then we are at the place of the open doors.

Where else is the presence of God to be found? In Mark 13:11 Jesus tells us:

> Whenever you are arrested and brought to trial, do not worry beforehand about what to say. Just say whatever is given you at the time, for it is not you speaking, but the Holy Spirit.

God is to be found outside the temple in the place of persecution, which He transforms into the place of witness. More needs to be said about the presence of God and the mystery of revelation.

The doorspace of the kingdom looks like the wall in which it is set, and yet it is there. For insight can be a heaven-door when heaven opens and God speaks to us; it can be a seed-door when Jesus speaks to us through the everyday material things around us; it can be a demon-door when Jesus' interaction with the demonic shows us some of the spiritual reality at work behind the scenes. It can be a touch-door, or a word-door – we have to be open and aware to what is going on around us at a deeper level.

We are forced by the mystery and paradox and hiddenness of the kingdom to examine ourselves – to become aware how deep the roots of the Word are in us or not (Mark 4:8). The change begins with us. If we have deep roots, we can be the one who perseveres until the end (Mark 13:13). We are marked as a disciple if we persevere until the end.

To fall awake into the vortex of the kingdom is real life – it is fullness of life; it enables us to see the beauty, the pain and the glory of life. Rowan Williams once wrote that Jesus was a person in whom the freedom of God was completely at work.[58] In the place of full awareness we see what the freedom of God is. We have removed the obstacles within us that restrict that freedom, and we allow that freedom to be at work fully within us. Each moment we live we ask, what is the freedom of God in this particular moment? And then we live it.

---

[58] Quoted in Rupert Shortt, *Rowan Williams: an Introduction* (London: DLT, 2003) p.65.

Day 35: Finding the doorspace

Read Mark 11; 12:1–13; 13

The mystery of the doorspace of the kingdom is that it is open but looks closed. It is the doorspace that moves to different places which we have to find, but it also teaches us to see that closed doors are not an obstacle and are to be sought out and passed through. We need to remember that the closed door of the tomb was forced open (Mark 16:4).

As we approach the final week, I want to try and summarise some of the key themes of the gospel of Mark as well as touch on some we have only alluded to. One such theme is that of conflict. There are many conflict stories in Mark. In our world of experiential avoidance we like to steer clear of conflict, or sweep it under the carpet. What seems to be part of the way of discipleship in Mark as modelled by Jesus is that conflict is sought out.

This is not about conflict for conflict's sake but about finding the places where truth and justice are distorted and bringing the truth in, opening the door of the kingdom in that place or looking for the hidden door of the kingdom in the place of conflict.

One of those places of conflict is to do with the Temple. The Temple was one of those things that the people of God took for granted to be solid and dependable and would always be there. Mark 13 begins with an unnamed disciple commenting with awe on the apparent indestructibility of the Temple – showing that he has not understood Jesus' cleansing of the Temple or His cursing of the fig tree as an enacted parable of the barrenness of the Temple.

One of the big themes in the last few chapters of Mark is the idea of Jesus as the cornerstone of the new Temple (Mark

12:10) with the Markan community also replacing the Temple as a 'house' of prayer (Mark 11:22–26). Jesus has overturned the tables in the Temple, condemned it for not being a house of prayer and cursed the fig tree, which is a symbol of the 'barren' Temple. He then talks about prayer: 'Therefore I tell you, whatever you ask for in prayer, believe that you have received it, and it will be yours' (Mark 11:24). Many misunderstandings about this verse would clear up if we understand the 'you' in this verse to be plural, corporate, the new community of prayer that is to replace the Temple.

What Jesus is doing here is the difference between being a peacemaker (Matthew 5:9) and a peace lover. A peacemaker goes into the places of distortion and injustice and brings the peace of justice and love and truth. A peace lover says there is peace where there is no peace, and avoids conflict.

At a relationship level, what Jesus has to say about conflict is also very important. He shows us this principle in Mark but spells it out in Matthew. We are not to do conflict indirectly, seeking to trap people, or talking about them behind the scenes (like the religious leaders in Mark). We are to go and talk to people face to face (Matthew 18:15).

All conflict is costly. Being a peacemaker is costly. Mark's challenge to us is enormous. Are we going to risk our own self to save others or are we going to fearfully save our own self? None of us know what we will do in extreme circumstances. I can say that this is the ethics of Jesus in Mark, but I haven't experienced it.

Of Gods and Men is a film based on a true story of seven monks known as the Atlas Martyrs who died together in Algeria. In the midst of a civil war one of the factions declared in 1993 that all foreigners needed to leave the country or face death. The monks chose to stay. The elderly monk who was the doctor, tending the local Muslim inhabitants, says in the film, 'I'm not scared of death. I'm a free man.' That's a good definition of the freedom we all strive for. However, the beauty of the film is in the way it explores the internal conflict of the monks: do they stay and face almost certain death, or do they leave? They stayed because they believed they were called to stand in the place of service and to be servants in that place, Algeria.

I hear people say glibly in the West that they would never run away or betray Jesus, but the reality is that such struggles are much more bitter than we might naively believe in our over-confident way. We have just never been fully tested. Mark's gospel sets out the way of being fully tested.

Week Six

Day 36: The riddles of learning

(in personal conversation with Professor Guy Claxton)

Mark's gospel is full of riddles and paradox. One of the deep principles of Guy Claxton's learning philosophy is about holding balances in creative tension. This should be one of the deep principles of the theology of learning within Christianity. Professor Claxton's commitment to balances held in creative tension comes from cognitive science's research into the structure of the mind, what he calls 'hare brain and tortoise mind'.

This balance between the fast, rational part of our brains, much favoured in Western culture, and the slower, more intuitive aspect of our minds, needs to be held in creative tension. Rational intelligence, when it is the dominant mode of thought, is not always the best way to solve problems.

'We need to hold a balance between rigour and reverie, thinking fast and decisively and also being able to think slowly and hesitantly,' says the professor. 'There's a balance to be struck between imagination and deliberation, perseverance and flexibility. It is a very important twenty-first-century life skill to know when not to do something. It's important to be trusting and it's very important in today's world to be sceptical about what you are being told.'

Research shows that innovation in business, science, schools and organisations comes out of holding these balances in creative tension. Congregations also aspire to be learning communities and require creative and innovative thinking to thrive in our ever-changing culture.

One biblical scholar has argued recently that God is entrepreneurial, and we are made in His image. Because of this we actually have creative kingdom opportunities in the midst of even an economic crisis, which cannot be solved with the same level of thinking that caused the mess in the first place.

Jesus Himself held balances in creative tension. He was both humble servant and authoritative leader, creative communicator and reliant on the Spirit.

Professor Claxton's thesis is that in education we have neglected more intuitive, implicit, tacit ways of knowing that are part of intelligence in favour of being smart, rather than clever. If we look at how Jesus encouraged learning by hiding truth and revealing it in parables and riddles, these more informal ways of knowing are part of our heritage – although probably not part of our own teaching from pulpits and in colleges.

Paul talks about praying with our minds and also praying with our spirits. Tongues is perhaps a vehicle for accessing the more intuitive part of our minds which are slow, and where God can speak to us more easily than in hare brain. I think we prefer praying with our minds in church and have neglected praying with our spirits.

A cognitive scientific riddle is that intelligence increases as we think less. Taking time off from thinking releases creativity. Contemplation is making a comeback in the church and is about doing nothing in order to change your life. A disposition to enjoy contemplation should be encouraged from the earliest age. Contemplative children's ministry is not a contradiction in terms but a glorious possibility.

The creative catalyst in the church should be the teaching pastor who demonstrates that he is a learner alongside his learning congregation. The wise pastor knows all about balances held in creative tension; whether it is the balance between milk and meat in preaching, order and spontaneity in worship, or balancing the needs of young and old, male and female, black and white within the congregation.

It is the pastor's most creative role to banish fear through fearless preaching – because fear inhibits creative thinking. Filled with the courage of the Holy Spirit, he demonstrates that we are resilient enough to fail and not give up, to persevere and give up judiciously. The congregation that is released from fear then has the divine spark of creativity released in them. Jesus in Mark seeks to banish the wrong kind of fear (Mark 4:40).

As a final plea, we need to restore the balance between being purpose driven and openly playful. The church as a sign of the inbreaking kingdom, which is the power from the future breaking into the present, should be a deeply playful and fun place to be. Righteous meanness should be banned and laughter and forgiveness and love given their rightful place as the truest history of humanity.

Day 37: The spiritual relationship on the street

One of the important themes in Mark is the relationship Jesus has with the Temple. One of the reasons Jesus was crucified is that He did out in the streets what was supposed to be done in the Temple by the priests.[59]

On Saturday 10th January 2009, at 11 o'clock in the morning, a team from Stanmore Baptist Church began praying for people outside Sainsbury's in the middle of Stanmore for two hours. We handed out flyers, put out three chairs and a five-metre banner which simply said, 'healing'.

Since then a team has been praying every week, come rain, snow or sunshine. What we have experienced has caused our thinking about healing, witnessing and the calling of the church to completely somersault.

We have had hundreds of prayer requests, handed out thousands of flyers and built some amazing relationships. People have been healed in many different ways. Some have come to church, become Christians, and been baptised. We have prayed for Jews, Hindus, Muslims, agnostics, rugby league supporters on their way to Wembley, and even some Christians!

Some people from Jewish and Hindu backgrounds come back almost every week for prayer.

We came across the Healing on the Streets model at the New Wine Christian family conference in the summer of 2008. It has been pioneered by an evangelist called Mark Marx who is based in Causeway Coast Vineyard, Coleraine, and his model has spread rapidly across the United Kingdom and Europe since Easter 2005.

---

[59] Insight gleaned from Revd Dr Crispin Fletcher-Louis, in a lecture.

That very first weekend Mark Marx came and did some training before leading us out on the street. The model is very simple and gentle, and anyone thinking of starting such a ministry should undergo his training. It is not about being weird or standing over people like a traffic cop with a hand stretched out. Before they begin, everyone in the team kneels to pray. When someone sits down for prayer, two of the team will kneel down next to them.

When we began, I think there were a lot of fears and anxieties within the team, but there has been very little overt hostility from the public and a lot of warmth and interest. In fact, most of the scepticism has come from other Christians. We now also offer tea and coffee to passers-by and many people are keen to open conversations with the team. Some people have stopped and watched transfixed as they see peace steal over people's faces as they are prayed for.

Others watch from a distance for a long time before coming for prayer because they are impressed that the team is there every week, even when it is below freezing.

What we have rediscovered is that the word 'healing' needs to be used in its broadest biblical sense. The same word in the New Testament is used for healing and salvation. The greatest healing of all is, of course, salvation, and both Christian healing and salvation are first and foremost about Christ. That is why we always pray in Jesus' name. One of the most amazing things is the way people's eyes fill with tears when we tell them that God loves them.

The sense we had was that a major and often forgotten part of Jesus' ministry was to go out of the Temple and do things that the priests wanted to keep in the Temple. As churches we often recreate a temple ministry where we expect people to come to us. In Harrow, which is one of the most religiously and ethnically diverse boroughs in London, that policy no longer works; we need to go to them.

What we have found is that as we step out in the unpredictability of the street, God gently leads people to wholeness through the prayers of the team. Part of the healing is that people are being listened to and attended to with respect and love. Many people comment about experiencing a peace or a love that we would call God's presence.

In Mark 6:7 we read this: 'Calling the Twelve to him, he sent them out two by two and gave them authority...' When we go out – and this is another mark of discipleship – we are given authority. In verse 13 we are told, 'They drove out many demons and anointed many sick people with oil and healed them.' This authority comes with what has been called the contagious holiness of God (or a good spiritual radioactivity), His potent presence to heal and cleanse. In Mark's gospel Jesus touches a leper (Mark 1:40–45) who is unclean by the understanding of the day; a woman who has been bleeding touched Him (Mark 5:25–34), who is unclean by the understanding of the day; and then Jesus touches a dead body (Mark 5:41), also unclean by the understanding of the day. He should be made unclean by these acts, but instead, as with the woman, 'power' (Mark 5:30) – His contagious holiness – went out of Him and makes that which was unclean clean. He touches these people in the order their afflictions appear in Numbers 5:2.

We must be prepared to go out on the street with that power and presence of God, to lose our cool life and find something much better.

Day 38: More on the real relationship with learning

(a personal conversation with Professor Guy Claxton)

We are to persevere to the end in a world that is not safe (Mark 13:13). John the Baptist served God and lost his head (Mark 6:27). We need to learn resilience. We also need the watchfulness of a mind alive. A mind alive is one that has the resilience to learn new things and unlearn old things.

Resilience is one of the key learning muscles that every person needs to exercise. It is not just ordinary people who need to learn new things and unlearn old things; it is also those Professor Claxton calls the clever-stupid-important people in government.

He makes the point that the National Literacy Strategy for primary schools which ran for a number of years was designed to raise standards of reading. However, the net effect of it, according to research, is that students' ability to read has gone up slightly while their disposition to read has gone down markedly.

'It's fairly clear,' he says, 'that turning reading into a stressful drudgery at school has a negative impact on young people's enjoyment of reading.'

What government needs to learn is that skills are not more important than the disposition to learn, and by encouraging the disposition to learn, skills are much more easily acquired.

If we encourage the disposition to learn, what we will begin to see is learning miracles – people previously dismissed as failures suddenly becoming creative inquisitive learners. Without resilience as a learning muscle, children and adults cannot cope with failure and so often give up trying to learn, or believe that they are not learners.

This is compounded by the dominant belief in fixed ability. As I said earlier, someone labelled as having a 30-watt mind and told they will never be any brighter, and that they are stupid, will no longer believe they can be a learner.

In our culture of rapid change and economic crisis, everyone needs to believe they can learn new things and unlearn old things. There is no longer any such thing as a job for life; our career paths will look more like crazy paving.

The word 'stupid' needs to be unlearnt, unmade, and its ruin smote amongst the rocks. Professor Claxton is deeply empathic to the pain of people who have been labelled in this way. When children and adults are released from the straitjacket of belief that they are 'stupid', then personal healing and learning miracles begin to happen.

Catherine of Siena (1347–1380) was one such learning miracle. She had been called an unlearned learner. Unable to read and write as a young woman, she learned these skills very quickly. She and her letters are deeply admired still today. As a learner she was a mind ahead of her time, disputing as a woman with bishops and popes in a patriarchal society. She was one of these frail threads of God that began to unravel the idea that women and learning do not go together.

Brother Anthony of Worth Abbey told me about Cardinal John Henry Newman, who only just scraped through his degree at Oxford. Qualifications, or the lack of them, do not tell the whole story of a person's learning capacity. It is something we need to unlearn.

We need to look at the person and not the bits of paper they present to us. When Newman set up a University in Dublin, it was first and foremost about producing a fully rounded person.

The theology of learning within Christianity has at its heart the belief that no one should ever be written off. Paul says that we can be 'filled to the measure of all the fulness of God' (Ephesians 3:19). We should believe that of everyone.

Also central to a Christian theology of learning is the idea of unlearning. Paul says in Romans 12:2, 'Do not conform any longer to the pattern of this world.' He goes on to say that we need to be 'transformed by the renewing of [our] mind'.

In Mark, the disciples have to unlearn the things of men (Mark 8:33) and learn the things of God. They were unlearned men and in the end became learning miracles.

Day 39: The distortion of narcissism revisited

If Jesus were to address narcissism in today's culture, He would do two things. Firstly He would tell a parable.

The Ukuc bird looked in the clear pond, saw her reflection and fell in love with it. 'The world revolves around me and mine,' she said.

The Ukuc bird whispered to the egg growing inside her, 'You will be the centre of all things...' She laid him in the nest of the reed warbler, in the middle of four warm, smaller eggs.

The little reed warbler returned, sensing a shadow in the sky. There were still four warm eggs in the nest. On the day the eggs hatched she was ecstatically happy. The big one in the middle demanded a lot of food. Each time she came back there was one chick fewer in the nest. Soon there was only one, who filled the nest, insatiably demanding food and attention.

One day Robin Redbreast, king of the birds, came to the Ukuc bird in a dream. She saw her baby proudly filling the nest of the reed warbler, and the little bodies lying on the floor below the nest of the reed warbler.

'Because you have reversed the true order of things, from now on your name will be reversed,' said the Robin. 'And that will be your cry and a warning to all other birds.'

The narcissist is like the cuckoo – there is only room for him in the nest. We need to offer a Christian critique of our narcissistic culture, and also some practical help.

The study of narcissistic leaders is big news, especially in the world of work. A recent successful film was *Horrible Bosses* – but fact is stranger than fiction. You may be a Christian who works for a horrible boss. What does it look like to work for someone who believes there is only really room for them in the nest, and what can you do about it?

Working for a narcissistic boss, you walk on eggshells. It disorientates because normal rules of relating do not apply. Your boss will take credit for any creative ideas you have. He will be suspicious and suspect your motives. Attacking and blaming others is his first form of defence at the slightest real or imagined hint of criticism. He will know what buttons to press in order to make you live with a constant sense of insecurity.

He will undermine you and others behind the scenes in order to make his position stronger. It may be that if he considers you unimportant, just a cipher, he will use you to do the menial work he is too important to do. It's as if reality is being rewritten around you.

This may sound far-fetched, but the literature on narcissism is full of horrific real-life stories of just such behaviours.

So what can you do about a boss like this? There are probably three main strategies to follow:

You can just walk away and leave your job. This is hard to do in today's economic climate.

You can try a strategy of appeasement. Your boss will spot this and walk all over you. With this strategy you may be put in a position where you are asked to compromise yourself ethically, because your boss thinks normal rules don't apply to him.

A third strategy is to use company rules and policies to try and contain the narcissist's behaviour. Keep clear written records of conversations and meetings. If at all possible, involve other people in the meetings as witnesses. If a number of you are treated unfairly, you can form a coalition – stand up together. In a church setting you can ensure, as far as possible, that proper process is followed. This is where a church constitution and principles of shared power and decisions made by consensus can be very helpful as a way of containing a power-hungry narcissist.

There may come a time when even these strategies don't work. At some point I think the ethics of Mark's gospel come into play. In Mark we are told that the way of the world is the fearful saving of self (Mark 8:35). This is the way of the world and human thinking, the way of appeasement or walking away.

The thinking of God that we are called to emulate is to risk our lives for others, to courageously put our heads on the block, to stick our necks out (Mark 8:35). The gospel is about tackling injustices and distortions in the world, including the world of work. That may cost us our job. This is the way of following Jesus. Because the second thing Jesus would do is turn the tables on narcissism.

Day 40: Repairing the relationship with business

Within His parables Jesus, consistently takes ordinary everyday things and events as the 'visible' focus of the riddle. It might be wineskins (Mark 2:22), ears of corn (Mark 2:23), a strong man's house (Mark 3:27), mother and brothers (Mark 3:31), a boat (Mark 4:1), seed (Mark 4:4), a lamp and its stand (Mark 4:21), pigs (Mark 5:11), loaves and fish (Mark 6:30–44), dogs (Mark 7:27), yeast (Mark 8:15), a blind man (Mark 8:22), a little child (Mark 9:36), salt (Mark 9:50), a camel (Mark 10:25), a colt (Mark 11:2), a fig tree (Mark 11:13), a vineyard and tenants (Mark 12:1–12), a denarius (Mark 12:15), the cock crowing (Mark 13:35; 14:72), bread and cup (Mark 14:22–23). But in this use of the visible, Jesus is also affirming the material world in which we live – His is not an otherworldly spirituality. That means we need to go into every part of the material world.

'The man walked by the church on the other side of the street without even seeing it.' This dream my wife was given about the church where we minister was a wake-up call. With the church building in the middle of a residential area, I knew we had to find a space in the local high street that would help make the church visible again.

As a church, we were standing on a threshold, as 'come to us' was no longer working so well, and we did not know what 'go to them' looked like. This holding place between two spaces has been called a 'liminal' space. Our previous role had become fragile, and our new role had not yet evolved.

I felt as though anything could happen. What did happen in response to the dream was that we began a process of setting up a cafe in the high street. This was a profound theological challenge. What business is it of a church to trade? However, we knew it had to be a business, a genuine business, with a subversive and distinctively Christian relational edge.

There is a theologically established paradigm of workplace ministry, but church and business in partnership seems to me to be a liminal threshold, undergoing rapid and important evolution.

Before I went into the pastoral ministry I worked for Lloyds Bank for ten years. My last job was as a Business Banking Manager in a small business centre. When I trained at Spurgeon's College I was encouraged to reflect theologically on that business experience. More recently I have been impacted by a new strand (to me) of business theology, which is different to workplace ministry, called 'Business As Mission' (BAM).

This paradigm has gained ground since the launch of the BAM manifesto at the Lausanne movement's Forum for World Evangelisation (LFWE) 2004 conference in Pattaya, Thailand.

What is 'Business As Mission'? Firstly, like any other business it exists to make profits and create wealth. But it has a wider purpose than that, which can be summarised through what is called a 'quadruple bottom line'. Unlike most businesses which operate with just a financial bottom line, a BAM business also operates with kingdom, social and environmental bottom lines.

Working with a kingdom bottom line means that although 'the business of business is business', BAM is business with a 'kingdom of God purpose and perspective'. This is not the same as business for mission, where businesses are used to fund what is seen as the 'real' ministry elsewhere.

The theological grounding of this movement is very important. It is argued that the idea of business itself as a force for good comes out of God's creation mandate. The good includes the creation of jobs – real jobs, which add more value than aid alone.

The hard thing to grasp, perhaps, for many Christians, is the idea that God is at work in and has a purpose for business.

Business, especially at a multinational level, does not have a good press. But we need to remember that Adam and Eve were created to work, and Jesus Himself was a businessman.

In a time of global recession, BAM is a movement whose time has come, as it seeks to help Christian entrepreneurs, both men and women, set up kingdom-focused transformational businesses.

Why is this urgent? Once kings controlled economies, then governments controlled economies, and now businesses are in control of economies. We have seen what happens when businesses are run without an ethical foundation, but historically we know through the example of Quaker businessmen and others that business can change communities.

Businessmen like George Cadbury saw mission as holistic, with no divide between sacred and secular, spiritual and physical. The BAM manifesto has incorporated this important theological principle into its theology. Business men and women are part of the whole church taking the whole gospel to the whole world.

I was interviewed at Spurgeon's College by Bill Allen, then a tutor, who tried to persuade me to stay in business. Serving God full-time in pastoral ministry is not the top of the pyramid. If you are called to be a businessman or woman there is no higher calling. Follow the call.

The Gnostic heresy which says spirit is good and the physical bad still taints the theology of business. The church needs to eradicate this heresy, which has its roots in Plato's dualistic thinking. What needs engaging with is the biblical, Hebraic idea that the material and spiritual form a unified whole. This Old Testament theological root can transform the tree of business into a tree of life full of God's wisdom.

This holistic thinking can be found in the Wisdom literature of Proverbs. Proverbs says the wisdom of God is woven into the natural and social order of the world. This includes the world of business. The wife of noble character at the end of Proverbs is a skilled business woman commended as full of God-woven practical wisdom.

When they were younger, our children used to enjoy 'joining up the dots' pictures. The wisdom of Proverbs is the fruit of meditating on the natural and social order of the world, 'joining up the dots' of wisdom that God has placed in the world.

This means business can be redeemed and run with God's practical wisdom. Wisdom is also imaged as a human being and a woman in order to convey that all of reality is relational and interconnected.

Because of this, business should not be disconnected from this spiritual and relational interconnectedness. The damage that unethical businesses inflict relationally, socially and environmentally demonstrates this connectedness. Conversely, business can be used to transform society, hence the idea of having a quadruple bottom line.

Business has so much to do with money that it can be and is heavily tainted with Mammon as a spiritual reality, as well as the principalities and powers of this world. However, it can be invaded and transformed with kingdom reality. Just like churches, businesses will always have a shadow side – and the work of redeeming that shadow side never ends.

There is another theological root in the Old Testament that needs to influence our theology of business. This comes out of the fruitful reflections of Old Testament scholars in recent years on what it means to be made in the image of God.

Much of this new thinking has revolved around the theology of entrepreneurship. At a national level, thinkers to engage with include the Anglican scholar Crispin Fletcher-Louis. There is also a research and development initiative at the University of Cambridge called Transforming Business which is led by important Christian thinkers including Dr Peter Heslam and Dr Flint McGlaughlin.

One of the key findings from research into entrepreneurship is that pervasive creativity is at the core of those we would call entrepreneurs. One of the lessons out of fresh reflection on the first three chapters of Genesis is that God is pervasively and creatively and continuously involved in the natural and social orders that came out of the initial act of creation.

The creation can be imaged as God's start-up, and humanity is invited to join God's start-up. The divine artisan creates us to be His apprentices.

God could be said, therefore, to be an entrepreneur rather than a blind distant watchmaker. If we are made in His image then humanity is also called to be entrepreneurial. The calling was to move out of Eden and fill and subdue the wilderness around Eden, taking the cultivated Garden out into all the world.

Those involved with Transforming Business and the Business As Mission paradigm argue that entrepreneurship, especially in small and medium-sized businesses, can be a genuine antidote to poverty.

They also argue that it can influence peace-building. The incoming kingdom of God brings peace, in which trade has its place. Isaiah 60:5 declares, 'Your eyes will shine, and your hearts will thrill with joy, for merchants from around the world will come to you' (NLT).

The third argument in favour of entrepreneurship is that it will lead us out of economic meltdown. This means that small, medium and large churches can themselves encourage a spirit of entrepreneurship. Part of the thinking behind our church setting up a cafe in our high street was to find a creative way of using business to help poverty.

Coffee is usually grown in volatile areas and the farmers are often poor. We have linked up with a Christian coffee company called Ethical Addictions which buys directly from farmers in Tanzania and Brazil, with the farmers receiving at least Fair Trade prices, and often more than that.

Entrepreneurs are people who take a step of faith. That sounds to me like the way forward, because every crisis is also an opportunity.

One of the most difficult things about the church setting up a cafe was obtaining information from other churches who had done this before. Setting up a cafe as a small business person is complex enough, but as a church setting up a trading subsidiary, the complexities increase exponentially.

This problem of finding helpful pioneers in this area highlighted a key aspect of Business As Mission or Transforming Business thinking. Secular businesses are run competitively and there is little collaboration. One of the subversive and distinctive aspects of BAM is the importance of collaboration.

Collaboration has its theological roots in the creation accounts of Genesis 1–3. One of the puzzling statements is the 'let us' of Genesis 1:26. 'Let us make man in our image' could be an implicit Trinitarian reference, or it could refer to the heavenly council of angels (as in Isaiah 6:2).

The important theological implication is that God consults others, that there is interaction, dialogue, a collaboration of some kind. Only God does the creating, but there is collaboration. God also invites human beings to collaborate with Him in His start-up; it is not a competition.

Fortunately we found a collaborative entrepreneur in nearby Watford. There is BAM thinking and practice going on at a local level as well as a national level. We made contact with a coffee shop in Watford based in a retail shop called Presence, owned and run by a Christian businessman. The manager and owner have met up with us on a number of occasions and openly shared key information in a collaborative way to help us with our start-up.

There are also a number of other BAM initiatives in Watford focused on working collaboratively who have helped us. Workplace Inspired is a Watford-based organisation for Christians in the workplace and Christians in business. Out of this organisation The Kingdom Business School trains, mentors and supports Christian entrepreneurs.

One of the faculty from the Business School, the Revd Dr Bridget Adams, came and spoken to the cafe team about BAM, and also spoke at one of our church services.

Unfortunately, many churches and many individuals do not believe they have it within them to be entrepreneurial. One of the myths about entrepreneurs is that they are a personality-type like Lord Sugar – extrovert, aggressive and risk-taking. Research shows that entrepreneurship can be learnt and that the personalities of entrepreneurs are extremely varied. At the core of every entrepreneur is a pervasive creativity and the ability to systematically innovate.

This is also underlined by another key theological insight from Genesis. Other ancient Near Eastern texts from Egypt show that only the Pharaoh was considered to be the 'image of God'. In Genesis this idea is democratised: it is every person, all humanity, male and female, that is made in the image of God.

If God is the divine artisan, the first entrepreneur, and we are made in His image, then we all have the capacity to be entrepreneurial.

It has been suggested that entrepreneurs are people who are more aware, alert and attentive to the opportunities in business than other people. Christians steeped in contemplative prayer, which makes them 'alert' and watchful and able to read the signs of the times, should have a creative edge in the ability to be entrepreneurial!

Conclusion

The watching we are called to in Mark brings us to the place of freedom. In that place the freedom of God can be completely at work within us. We are fully aware of what God is doing and we follow Him (Mark 1:17).

It is not a passive watching; it makes us still and still moving. I am intrigued with the sport known as free running. As I observe it I see that at its heart is a new type of seeing and awareness, an open attention which sees ordinary things in new ways: the top of a wall is not to keep us out but to run along; a stairwell is not for climbing but built for hurdling; a gap between two buildings is not to allow us to walk between them but to jump from one to the other. The watching we are called to is free watching – it sees new possibilities in ordinary things. It is the watching that enables us to see where the freedom of God is and move in it, even if it is into a place of persecution and suffering. That place of freedom is only to be found by paying full attention to the cross and resurrection of Jesus.

The women who follow Jesus watch the cross attentively from a distance (Mark 15:40). Then they draw close. Very close. At the tomb a young man speaks to them, the stone has been rolled away and the tomb is empty. He has a message from Jesus for them. The last words of the gospel are:

> Trembling and bewildered, the women went out and fled from the tomb. They said nothing to anyone, because they were afraid.
> *Mark 16:8*

This is often seen as a problematic ending. That somehow this is a failure on the part of the women as disciples. But

184

consider this: they become aware of their incompleteness in the light of the completeness of the resurrection atmosphere at the tomb; they become aware of their possible completeness as they are told to journey on with the male disciples to Galilee where they will 'see' Jesus (Mark 16:7).

In the presence of the fullness of the kingdom at the empty tomb, they know their emptiness and taste the fullness that one day will be theirs. What possible response could there be except *ekstasis* (Mark 16:8), from which we get our word ecstasy?

At the great unveiling of the kingdom at the empty tomb, what possible response could there be but silence? The whisper of suffering in the beginning of Mark ended in a shout (Mark 15:37), which cry of completion paves the way for the silence after the resurrection.

In the Book of Revelation, at the opening of the seventh seal, there was 'silence in heaven' (8:1). Seven is the number of perfection, and the silence at the tomb suggests the women had experienced the perfection of the kingdom.

I wonder if you have reflected on what happiness is in Mark's gospel. This is happiness – the coming alive of every aspect of our being, every particle within us dancing in the presence of the infinite, in the presence of God.

But there is more evidence than this. This experience at the tomb is one of true seeing which occurs many times in Mark's gospel. Whenever the kingdom of God comes near in its numinous awe in Mark, the same group of words we see in Mark 16:8 recurs in various forms.

When Jesus raises the 12-year-old girl from the dead in Mark 5:41–42, the same word *ekstasis* is used. Literally the Greek says, 'They were astonished immediately with a great astonishment.' This response of awe, reverential fear and trembling occurs again and again. At one point in chapter 9 Jesus appears, and Mark writes, 'As soon as all the people saw

185

Jesus, they were overwhelmed with wonder and ran to greet him' (verse 15). When the finite meets the infinite there is this response. When the two levels of reality – spiritual and material – are experienced simultaneously, there is this response. It's as if the location of the crowd has changed and yet it hasn't.

One of the paradoxical riddles in Mark is what Jesus says about inside and outside (Mark 4:11). At the empty tomb the women are inside the kingdom but are aware still of their outsideness – and yet they see their way to being fully inside. This is because they are in the right place, as close to Jesus as it is possible to be – at the place of the cross and the resurrection.

The perversion of our capacity to see, hear or know as God intends us to see, hear or know is the source of evil. The restoration of our capacity to see, hear or know as God intends is the beginning of our transformation. It is a lifelong journey and we must persevere to the end – finding the places where we can re-locate and re-orientate ourselves.

Mark tells us where these places are. The most challenging place is to put ourselves where suffering and persecution are, trusting the Holy Spirit to give us revelation in that moment (Mark 13:9–11). In these places the theology of Mark's watchfulness is a theology of being before doing. It is a theology of presence. Find the presence of God and be present as well. But Jesus is not just a doer in Mark's gospel; He shows us 'being' in all its fullness. He is a healing presence, a challenging presence, a mysterious presence – a presence full of God which leaves us in ecstasies, trembling in numinous awe.

We are called to be human in Mark' s gospel, in our frailty and in our perseverance and in our attachment to one another. We are called to be servants in our hearts before we do service. We can throw a net over Mark's gospel but we won't catch Jesus that way; we need to follow Him, as the bushman follows the honey bird to honey. And if we follow Him, we end up at the cross.

Mark has already told us what the meaning of the cross is: 'For even the Son of Man did not come to be served, but to serve, and to give his life as a ransom for many' (Mark 10:45). Jesus takes our place on the cross that we might take His place in the kingdom of His Father. Discipleship in Mark is entering into the freedom that we have been ransomed for, and leaving behind the slaveries we have been ransomed from. It requires watchfulness.

As we take up the place in the kingdom that Jesus has bought for us, we are given the mysterious authority of the kingdom (Mark 3:15). We are to learn this watchfulness in order to know how to live freely in the difficult present moment. We are assured of the future and of God's promises to us (Mark 13:31). We don't speculate about that future but we live in the light of it (Mark 13:32). Mark is also a book for this time in which we live, in all its uncertainty.

We need to breathe the atmosphere of Mark, which is made up of many little details. We need to read it and reread it as a whole, as well as pay attention to the detail. As we breathe it, we know we stand before God like parched earth in the presence of near rain – expectant, waiting.

We find the way in doing our daily tasks, while watching, watching for the free-running God, that we might allow His freedom to run in us. In that freedom we form a continuous working relationship with God that is prayerful; we correct distortions within ourselves and the world around us; we find our real selves; and we are part of the repairing new creation of the kingdom that has come near.

The mindFullness we can experience as Christians includes being filled with the fullness of the kingdom, the very presence of God. As Jesus says mysteriously 'the kingdom of God is within you' (Luke 17:21). It is being set free from the cravings of the empty self, which is shaped in the patterns of this world. It is freedom to love courageously, because there is no courage in defensive anger – only fear. Courage comes out of love.

The God we worship is an aware God, omniscient as we say. Jesus was aware and attentive. He modelled that for us and, made in the image of God, we too have the capacity to be aware and attentive, and for that inner capacity to be transformed. Our hearts can be stretched with love to include our neighbours and our enemies, and in awareness we can gaze on them with the same love with which God gazes on them.

The ancient spiritual disciplines of *Lectio Divina* and the Jesus Prayer take us into the place of transformation where God's grace can work.

As we engage with Mark's gospel, the key insight we glean is that we see in a distorted and sinful way. That is why we need to be watchful. Becoming watchful is learning to see straight, and true and far, both the seen and the unseen that make up the reality that faces us. Mark wants us to be reality-focused.

Silence and solitude take us into the place where we can listen, hear and pay attention to the presence of God. In fact, at the end of Mark's gospel, the women at the tomb were filled with silent awe (16:8). They were mind*Full.*

A study guide for leaders' and participants using *A Book of Sparks* as a six-week course

A number of churches and small groups have used *A Book of Sparks* as a resource for a six-week course. Out of discussions and involvement with them I have produced this study guide, which will enable anyone reading the book or leading a small group to run a course introducing Christian mind*Full*ness. I have also recorded six podcasts that are available at http://shaunlambert.co.uk/. Using these weekly enables you to draw out the maximum benefit during the 40 days.

During this period you can also explore the daily guided meditations to be found in the mindfulness-based and mindfulness-incorporating therapies. There are plenty of free resources on the web, including at www.franticworld.com/free-meditations-from-mindfulness/.

Slow reading of *A Book of Sparks*
Encourage everyone to read one chapter a day, slowly and with attention, and to do the spiritual practices suggested. Invite people to come back to the section in the introduction on mindful reading, until the principles become part of them.

Paying attention wherever we are
The book looks at different aspects of the world to help us pay attention wherever we are.

Other resources
At the end of the study guide, I will suggest other resources to help people engage. Most of these can be printed. These include a radio interview, helping men engage, families and

children, and drawing out the often hidden creative gifts people have for poetry, art, etc.

Preparation
We are tracking the journey of Jesus and the disciples from the beginning of the gospel through to the cross and resurrection. It is our journey too.

Mark's gospel was originally an oral gospel, to be listened to as a whole, not just read. We have found that encouraging people to listen to it as a whole, or to long sections, is very helpful. The best 'performance' of it is the DVD of Max McLean's complete rendition of it on stage.[60]

Suggestions:
- Have an evening where you watch it together.

- Play sections during a Sunday service.

- Encourage house groups to watch it.

Weekly guide

Week One
I outline at the beginning of the book that change and transformation are at the heart of Christian discipleship. This is the creation of a new mind in us – one that is Christlike. Much of modern discipleship is about the giving of information, but information by itself does not transform.

The question to ask is, 'Yes, but how?' What is it that brings transformation? The answer is that transformation comes

---

[60] http://www.amazon.com/Marks-Gospel-Edition-Max-McLean/dp/B003B2XP10

through the meditative practices outlined in the book. These are what lay down new neural pathways in the brain.

Transformative discipleship begins in the mind, as we ask this riddle, 'Am I my thoughts and feelings?' (see pages 24-26). The meditative practices help us decentre from our thoughts and feelings, to move out of autopilot and into informed awareness. The key contemplative disciplines are *Lectio Divina* (a slow prayerful reading of Scripture) and the Jesus Prayer. Reinforce this in different ways, as the book does. Read out the introduction to *Lectio* to the group on pages 43-44.

Lectio Divina is different to Bible study. In *Lectio* you allow the God-breathed Word to stand over you, and you seek to lovingly internalise it.

In the introduction I say more about mindful reading. The daily meditations are written to be read mindfully, and to encourage mindful reading. As we begin to tune in to a more mindful way of being we can then apply that new seeing to ourselves and to the people and the world around us.

Whether you are in a discussion group or working through the book on your own, here are some questions to consider at the end of Week One:

- Have you come across mindfulness in your everyday life?

- People are often reluctant to change. Why do you think this is?

- The first realisation we need to make if we are going to change is that, like the disciples, we don't see or hear clearly. We are spiritually blind and deaf. The change that is required is one of perspective – we need to reperceive the world through God's eyes. Is this an insight you can work with?

- Summarise your understanding of mindfulness so far.

Week Two

This week the pregnant idea to discuss is that the battleground of change is in our minds, and the central insight of mindfulness or contemplation is that we are not our thoughts and feelings. In fact, we are bigger than our thoughts and feelings. Also our thoughts and feelings are not an accurate readout of reality.

With this insight we then use mindful awareness or meditative practices to look at our thoughts and feelings rather than looking at life from the point of view of our thoughts and feelings. As we do this, our relationship difficulties are suddenly seen in a new light.

One of the other key things that is being developed through the reading of the book is our relational awareness. Throughout the book we focus on five archetypal relationships: spiritual, real, working, distorted and wounded in need of repair.

Encourage people to share obstacles and encouragements from beginning this journey. What have they noticed about themselves? Have they noticed that God is involved in the little details of their life?

Invite them to write their own personal rhythm of life that builds in time for silence and contemplation. As well as first thing in the morning, just stepping out of clock time – for one minute or perhaps three minutes – can reconnect them to the presence of God.

Whether you are in a discussion group or working through the book on your own, here are some questions to consider at the end of Week Two:

- Remind yourselves, what is the central insight of mindfulness?

- Where exactly does the battle for transformation in the Christian life take place? Requote Mark 1:15, Romans

12:2 and 2 Corinthians 10:5. Read pages 71-72 to help you reflect on this inner battle.

- Ask people if they can remember the key elements of the cognitive map outlined in the podcast: we learn to focus our attention, our mind wanders, we notice what it wanders to, we switch our attention back to ... our breath, the Jesus Prayer, the Scripture...

- Why not try a slow reading of Scripture now (*Lectio Divina*)? You could try Mark 1:35-39.

Week Three

A key value to reinforce is that the Christian life is a learning journey. We are mindful learners, not know-it-alls who treat others as know-nothings.

We also have a long biblical as well as historical tradition of valuing being and not just doing. It is important to shift from what psychologists call the doing mode – rational critical thinking, to the being mode – the place of awareness and intuition within.

This is something Jesus valued. I think that's why He spoke in parables. Parables, with their use of riddling and ambiguity, help us shift out of our normal patterns of thinking.

Another way of saying this is to underline the importance of finding still waters within, and also of going out into creation and into art galleries, etc. Encourage people to share creative stories of how they pray. Encourage them to journal, to 'track' their afflictive thoughts, to be prepared to be open and vulnerable. The Jesus Prayer is an important discipline in this 'tracking', and it also enables people to walk in the footsteps of the Invisible One (God).

Whether you are in a discussion group or working through the book on your own, here are some questions to consider at the end of Week Three:

- Try to think of ways you are stuck in doing rather than being? How might you shift to the being mode?

- Reread pages 94-96 out loud and slowly, maybe more than once. Practise really allowing it to sink in.

- We looked at the parable of the seed and the sower in Mark 4:1-9. What emerged for you as you engaged with this?

- I also talked about the importance of perseverance, of staying with the practices. This is often what people find most difficult. Why is this? People doing this course have said things like:
  'I feel guilty if I stop and do nothing.'
  'I think I'm being selfish if I take time for renewing my own sense of self.'

- One way to find the motivation to do these practices daily is to find the reason for doing it. What is the intention that would motivate you?

Don't forget that we have recorded a separate download for you, talking you through mindful walking.

Week Four

In ironic contrast to the disciples in Mark's gospel, Jesus is the master and commander of attention. Mark 8–9 is very important here. Try to notice your own patterns of anxious, competitive and suspicious watching. Can you replace these with Jesus' way of watching, seeing the world as if through the eyes of God, which is contemplation? We need to help people to realise the central message of Mark's gospel – that none of us see clearly.

In this session you can focus on the chapters on the Jesus Prayer. Reread pages 147-150.

Whether you are in a discussion group or working through the book on your own, here are some questions to consider at the end of Week Four:

- What do you remember of the biblical and historical background to the Jesus Prayer?

- The Jesus Prayer places an important emphasis on ensuring that the body and breath are part of our spiritual practices. How have you found using it?

- Use the story of blind Bartimeaus (Mark 10:46–52) as a *Lectio Divina*.

The Jesus Prayer can be used for longer periods of contemplation. Try it as a three-minute breathing space during your normal day – just to step out of clock time. Remember this practice shows us a Christian distinctive – mindfulness of the presence of God.

Other people using this course have begun to think creatively about their own informal mindfulness practices. These include a mindful bath, mindful stroking of the cat, even mindful walking of the dog!

Week Five
This week in the podcast we have been reviewing the main things we are trying to do when we're practising mindfulness or being contemplative.

The first thing is about learning to pay attention wherever we are. That's why the meditations in this book are wide ranging. There is no place where God is not, no place where we cannot track Him.

Whether you are in a discussion group or working through the book on your own, here are some questions to consider at the end of Week Five:

- Different ways of paying attention have been mentioned, whether it is nature writing, the *Lindisfarne Gospels*, using mindfulness informally through eating or cleaning your teeth. How could you practice mindfulness informally?

- In this fifth podcast I talk about the importance of mindful reading. What have you understood as the main difference between this and speed reading, or academic reading?

- All truth is God's truth, and I have been talking about the neuro-scientific evidence for how meditative or mindful awareness practices change our brain for the better. This is one of the central benefits of using these practices consistently. Remind yourself of this evidence now. Do some further research.

- What is your intention behind doing these practices? Is it mindfulness for health; is it to come into the presence of God; is it transformation? Or is it a combination of these things?

- Remind yourself of the mnemonic BOAC, and how it summarises the central ideas of being mindful.

- The disciples want to avoid the reality of the cross (p.140-142). Are we avoiding facing reality?

Reality-focused Christian contemplative or meditative practices are not just for us. All over the UK there is a spiritual awakening where people outside the church are looking for spiritual practices, and turning to psychology and Buddhism. We have an opportunity for contemplative evangelism!

Week Six
In this final week of the podcast, we focus again on the themes in the meditations for this week in the book We are also

emphasising that mindfulness can be used for health, and that it can have a Christian scaffolding.

In the book I have talked about the Christian distinctive of coming into the presence of God using spiritual practices like *Lectio Divina* and the Jesus Prayer. Through the varied meditations we have seen how it is important to pay attention wherever we are: each moment is sacred, a sacrament, a gift from God.

But there is also the scaffolding of a Christian way of life, and in this last podcast I talk about the Benedictine vows of stability, change and listening obedience.

Whether you are in a discussion group or working through the book on your own, here are some questions to consider at the end of Week Six:

- What might this Christian scaffolding look like for you? Where do you need to bring in stability? Where do you need to change? Where do you need to practise listening obedience?

- We are moving away from fear and towards freedom and compassion towards ourselves, others and creation. Using the Ananias Prayer, think about what it is that you find difficult in yourself that you need to face, and what is it in someone else – an enemy, someone you don't like – that you need to face?

- Review again the key insights that you have gleaned from this course.

- How can you begin to watch in a new way that is not shaped in the patterns of this world, a way that is not suspicious, anxious and fearful, competitive, acquisitive?

- How can you help each other, or yourself, to live consistently in these practices, and in community?

Perhaps you can text each other a reminder to practise each day?

Bring out the importance of slowing down, and the importance of reclaiming our bodies within our spiritual practice. Emphasise that the cross and resurrection are the place of the fullest revelation for us.

How can we go out into the world taking the contagious presence of God? Healing on the streets? Entrepreneurial adventures?

Have we lost the sense of wonder and numinous awe (*ekstasis*)?

Afterwards
Follow up with a Quiet Day or a retreat for the church.

Flat Earth Unroofed
a tale of mind lore

Shaun Lambert

Chapter 1
Hudor
and the Palimpsest of Bentley Wood

So it began here, with a forgetting of colour, the colour of flight. It began with the woodpecker dead on the grass in the back garden beneath the apple tree, its wings nailed to the ground, the wind ripping them apart. No more would grass grow under where it lay. He did not know whether this death was aimed at him, whether it was a random act of cruelty, or whether it was aimed at all of nature. Green and red feathers were dimmed by death, no more a laughing call, or swooping flight, or the prediction of rain. That was only the first sign. Storm.

The white hare danced, boxing outside his window. He knew it could not be so. He was in a waking dream, a dream so real it was as though the hare was fighting an invisible foe, and white fur tinged with blood flew in the air. In the dream awake he saw the ordinary street, cracked pavements, tarmac road, grass verge, houses and gateways begin to dissolve, and a nothingness was there. But in the ordinariness he saw gold shining, and he knew it was the end of all things. He got up at once to run but a voice said, 'Write and draw what you watch, where you walk, in your lane and beyond as far as you can. Watch and write and draw what you capture on water-marked paper. For that will preserve the warp of your world against that which comes, and those who come. Watch those who make a weakening of the self, for they are walking. Learn to hide your whole self.'

As he awoke, he felt an emptiness and an aching loss within his heart and he knew that he had heard true. Outside his window was the apple tree, the dead patch in the grass, and beyond that the high wire fence to the school field. But it was quiet outside. It was not a school day.

He dressed quickly and went outside into the front garden. By the road, against the hedge, a white hare trembled. It did not resist his hands, and it was like a knowing from his dream that he was to put her – for the eyes told him it was a female – in his satchel. The eyes looked human. He thought he saw an old man dressed in black on the corner of the road – the man with the scarred, marred face who lived in Bentley Wood. But when he looked again there was no one there. He felt irrationally guilty and wondered if he had been seen, but all that was there was a robin on the rubbish bin.

Everywhere there were people who worked for the Fowler. The Fowler had recently banned parents from teaching their own children. Every child now had to go to a controlled school.

He began to walk along the road on his way to Bentley Wood. The Wood had other names but these had been defaced. He thought he might release the hare there. As he turned the corner of the lane, he jumped. The old man was there looking at him. He found it hard to look at his face, but the eyes were kindly.

'Need to learn how to hide yourself, I reckon,' said the old man. Part of him wanted to stop and ask him why he said that, but he kept on walking, giving him a surprised sideways look as he went.

'Go to Friend's Meadow,' said the old man quietly. And then he was gone.

He always felt better amongst the ancient woodland. Friend's Meadow felt too close to the approach road and the houses so he went further into the woods. He followed the meadow that ran between the two sections of woodland, as if he was following an invisible line on the ground. He was being pulled to the left and to the top of this ancient piece of land.

Suddenly he could sense the rich smell of cow dung. The ghost cattle had been in this part recently. They were called ghost cattle because they had the ability to appear suddenly without being noticed.

He felt he should stop at the spring that bubbled up into a shallow pond. He knew for a moment that he was safe and not being watched. He knelt down and carefully took the white hare out of his bag. The hare looked at him calmly. He carefully washed the blood out of its fur, but there seemed to be no wound; it was as if the water had healed the wound.

The hare watched him with onyx eyes. Out of the corner of his eye he saw two other hares appear, watching him. He was still. He noticed that the cut on his thumb had gone when he had put it in the water.

He knew the hare had wanted him to see this. He could not explain it to himself, but he felt in that moment as if he knew something, as if he knew they were ancient watchers. In watching, they were guarding something, something they had shown him. And then they were gone.

He knew it was time to go home. It wasn't good to linger and draw attention to this place. He went home via a different route, picking up conkers as he walked to give himself a reason for being out.

As he walked home he thought about the old man. Mac, he was known as. Hudor knew that he worked in Bentley Wood below the big house. The big house was where the Master lived – the Fowler as the locals called him. Hudor was allowed in the Wood, which had open spaces and meadows and lakes, although it wasn't open – it was all fenced off. He was allowed in because his dad worked the guard dogs in the Wood. The old man, Mac, also helped with the dogs. He felt he should talk to Mac. He was excited about the white hares, but he didn't want to think about the woodpecker.

Hudor wished he were invisible. He could imagine his skin peeling off him if he were to be caught in the gaze of the Fowler.

He was where he shouldn't be, walking as stealthily as he could. He could hear his breathing and see his breath in the early morning frosty air. Suddenly somebody laughed, and he nearly jumped out of his shoes.

He looked around. A bird with a red crown and a green body walked round a tree trunk and out of sight. Hudor could see nothing else.

Hudor walked on; he needed to get to the top of the hill. Suddenly the green bird with the red crown undulated past him. It had a yellow rump. He heard the laugh again. It was the bird. The bird landed on the tree. 'Yaffle, yaffle,' it laughed.

As the bird laughed for the third time, Hudor was suddenly aware of black clouds gathering, faster than he had ever seen before. He needed to be quick.

It was then that the bird spoke. He would remember that moment for the rest of his life. As the clouds seemed to speed up, time around him seemed to slow down.

It was an oracle. He knew that now, but he didn't know it then. 'Follow the scryer to the path of the seed and the underwritten sentence or your soul lose…'

The bird turned its head and long beak to one side and looked at him with golden eyes and black pupils. Suddenly the eyes blazed with a light that left him with a longing in his heart for he knew not what.

And then it was gone. A green woodpecker! he thought. He didn't know there were any left. And one had died in his garden.

He was by now on top of the hill. In his vision it was a dark night, and there was no light pollution, only a clear sky streaming with starlight. Silence was all he could hear. His heart strummed with joy and his mind was as clear as the sky.

He was floating just a foot above the ground, pale clothed. He could see in front of him an open book. It was out of reach, but he knew he must find it in real life.

His eyes felt suddenly bright with light, and he could see that underwriting lay faintly on the upturned page. Overwriting in a different language and pen could also be seen.

He felt as though he was part of nature, his body humming with the music of every particle. But he also sensed a counter-vibration, something wrong, a storm coming. As he watched the sky, the moon began to turn red.

He remembered it all as if it were yesterday. Then he was back in this dimension, trying to get home without being seen, ordinary daylight all around him.

At supper he asked his father about Mac.

'Old Macarius?' said his Dad. 'Not all who wander are lost.'

This didn't help much, thought Hudor. He knew his dad liked to give short riddling answers, often from ancient books that had been lost.

'Yes, old Mac,' said Hudor.

'He's one of the last peregrini,' said his father. Hudor didn't like to ask more, but he didn't think calling him a falcon was particularly illuminating.

'Have a chat with him,' added his Dad, unexpectedly. Ask him to show you some of his — woodcraft.

'I will,' said Hudor, and he did.

Other resources[61]

Interview re silence and contemplation on UCB radio with Shaun Lambert
https://soundcloud.com/#ucbmedia/silence-and-contemplation

Sticky Faith – Noticing God. Resources for helping young people and families engage together
http://stickyfaith.org/

An ancient term for a contemplative was a 'tracker' – a word that helps men engage
http://www.instantapostle.com/blog/is-lent-for-men-rediscovering-the-lost-art-of-spiritual-bushcraft/

One-minute icons to help us step out of clock time during a busy day
http://shaunlambert.co.uk/2012/12/14/one-minute-icon-inner-sanctuary/

More on attention, awareness and mindfulness
http://www.mindandsoul.info/Articles/339737/Mind_and_Soul/Resources/Hot_topics/Mindfulness/A_Christian_perspective.aspx

More on the neuroscience of how God changes your brain
http://www.baptist.org.uk/Articles/370748/How_God_Changes.aspx

---

61 All websites in this section accessed 4 February 2014.

Suggested reading and bibliography

Books

Babiak, P. & R. D. Hare, *Snakes in Suits: When Psychopaths Go to Work*, London: Harper (2006)

Barrington-Ward, S., *The Jesus Prayer*, Oxford: BRF (2007)

Barrington-Ward, S. & Brother Ramon, *Praying The Jesus Prayer Together*, Oxford: BRF (2001)

Burnett, R., 'Mindfulness in Schools: Learning Lessons from the Adults, Secular and Buddhist' (October 2009)

Clarkson, P., *The Therapeutic Relationship*, London: Whurr Publishers Ltd (1995)

Claxton, G., *What's the Point of School*, Oxford: Oneworld Publications (2008)

Clement, O., *The Roots of Christian Mysticism*, London: New City (2002)

Clinebell, H., *Ecotherapy: healing ourselves, healing the earth*, London: The Haworth Press (1996)

Darlington, M., *Otter Country*, London: Granta (2012)

Diadochus of Photike, *Following the Footsteps of the Invisible: The Complete Works of Diadochus of Photike* (Introduction, Translation and Notes by Cliff Ermatinger), Collegeville, Minnesota: Liturgical Press (2010)

The Diagnostic and Statistical Manual of the Mental Disorders (DSM-IV-TR) Washington DC: APA, (2000)

Dodaro, R. & G. Lawless, *Augustine and his Critics: Essays in Honour of Gerald Bonner*, London: Routledge (2000)

Fry, T. (Ed.), *The Rule of St. Benedict in English*, Collegeville/Minnesota: The Liturgical Press (1982)

Grenz, S. J., *Theology for the Community of God*, Carlisle: Paternoster Press (1994)

Hollis, M., *The Boy on the Edge of Happiness*, Smith Doorstep (1996)

Jamison, Abbot C., *Finding Sanctuary*, London: Phoenix (2006)

Kets de Vries, M., *The Leader on the Couch*, Chichester: John Wiley & Sons Ltd (2006)

Laird, M., *Into The Silent Land*, London: DLT (2006)

Lambert, S., *Flat Earth Unroofed: a tale of mind lore* Watford: Instant Apostle (2013)

Langer, E., *The Power of Mindful Learning*, Addison-Wesley Publishing Co Inc (1997)

Lightfoot, R. H., *The Gospel Message of St Mark*, London: OUP (1950)

Locke, J. L., *Why We Don't Talk to Each Other Anymore – the De-Voicing of Society*, New York: Touchstone (1998)

McCown, D., D. Reibel & M. S. Micozzi, *Teaching Mindfulness*, Springer (2011)

Merton, T., *The Monastic Journey*, London: Sheldon Press (1977)

Newberg, A., & Waldman, M. R., *How God Changes Your Brain*, New York: Ballantine (2010)

Nicholson, W., *Firesong*, London: Egmont (2002)

Palmer, G. E. H., P. Sherrard & K. Ware (Eds.), *The Philokalia*, London: Faber & Faber (1979)

Playfoot, J. & R. Hall, *Effective Education for Employment*, Edexcel (2009)

Quicke, M., *360-Degree Preaching*, Grand Rapids Michigan: Baker Academic (2003)

Schnarch, D., *Passionate Marriage*, New York/London: W. W. Norton & Co (1997)

Seligman, M. E. P., *Authentic Happiness*, London: Nicholas Brealey Publishing (2003)

Shortt, R., *Rowan Williams: an Introduction*, London: DLT (2003)

Stewart, C. OSB, *Prayer and Community: The Benedictine Tradition*, London: DLT (1998)

Sugarman, L., *Life-Span Development*, Hove: Psychological Press Ltd (2001)

Van der Hart, W. & R. Waller, *The Worry Book*, Nottingham: IVP (2011),

Walker, S., *The Undefended Leader* Trilogy, UK: Human Ecology Partners (2011)

Walker, S., *The Undefended Life*, UK: Human Ecology Partners (2011)

Ward, B. (tr.), *The Desert Fathers: Sayings of the Early Christian Monks*, London: Penguin (2003)

West, C., *Theology of the Body for Beginners: A Basic Introduction to Pope John Paul II's Sexual Revolution*, West Chester, Pennsylvania: Ascension Press (2004)

Willard, D., *Renovation of the Heart*, Leicester: IVP (2002)

Williams, M., & D. Penman, *Mindfulness: A practical guide to finding peace in a frantic world*, Piatkus (2011)

Wolters, C. (tr.), *The Cloud of Unknowing and other Works*, Harmondsworth: Penguin, (1983)

Journals

Cambridge Papers

Clinical Psychology: Science and Practice

Contemporary Buddhism

Websites[62]

www.franticworld.com/free-meditations-from-mindfulness/
http://www.goldhillholidays.co.uk/
http://mindandsoul.info/
http://theleadershipcommunity.webeden.co.uk/
http://www.worthabbey.net/
http://shaunlambert.co.uk/
http://shaunlambert.co.uk/podcasts/
http://flatearthunroofed.com/

---

[62] All accessed 4 February 2014.